TRELAWNY of 1906 from a contemporary painting in the possession of Mr. L. G. Brown of Bristol.

HAIN OF ST. IVES

By K. J. O'Donoghue

&

H. S. Appleyard

Published by the World Ship Society
Kendal LA9 7LT
1986

CONTENTS

ISBN 0-905617-41-X

Printed by **Gibbons Barford Print,** Wolverhampton, England

ACKNOWLEDGEMENTS

Our thanks are extended to the many who helped in the preparation of this history. In particular, Kenneth Ingram who made available his extensive collection of Hain material; Stephen Rabson, P&O Librarian for access to the remaining company minute books and other documents; Dr David Jenkins, Research Assistant, Cardiff Industrial and Maritime Museum; Mrs P. Johnson and Stanley Cock, both of St. Ives, who on one of the wettest days imagineable opened up the Hain Rooms at St. Ives Museum especially for us. Thanks are also due to Len Sawyer, who contributed the paper on 'MAC' ships, Michael Crowdy, E. N. Taylor, Martin Benn, Alan Phipps, John Behenna, Bernard Lawley, Rowan Hackman, Tony Atkinson, R. Penhallurick, R. Hall, G. Smale and the Fleet Air Arm Museum, Yeovilton.

Where known, photographs have been credited to their photographer or the collection from which they were obtained. Unfortunately, a proportion of the photographs were lost during the preparation of the book and the origin of many is not known. Apologies if any are incorrectly captioned and thankyou to all those who responded so magnificently to the appeal for further views.

The frontispiece is from a painting in the collection of Leslie Brown of Bristol.

Reference has been made to the privately published memoirs of Sir George Christopher, one of the last Chairmen of the company.

Edward, later Sir Edward, Hain
1851-1917

THE HAIN STEAMSHIP CO. LTD.

Today's small Cornish fishing port of St. Ives seems an unlikely location as the birthplace of one of the major shipping companies of the late 19th century. Yet it was there that The Hain Steamship Company was founded, and from there it was controlled until the takeover by P&O in 1917.

The Hain family had long been resident in the town, and their name can be traced back to the 16th century. Their first recorded shipping venture would seem to be a part share in the fishing lugger DASHER, which was built and registered at St. Ives in 1816. Edward Hain (I), Michael Welch and Matthew Daniel, all described as mariners, took equal shares in the vessel. She was commanded by Edward Hain (I) until in 1832 he retired from the sea, although his shareholding was retained. The DASHER was successful, and on 17 February 1838 the schooner CAMILLA was purchased. This time control of the vessel was firmly in the hands of the Hain family, with 16 shares held by Edward Hain (I) and 32 shares held by his son Edward. The balance of the shares were held by Richard Paynter, a St. Ives fisherman whose family was closely connected with the Hains.

The CAMILLA was purchased from Thomas and William Bolitho of Gulval near Penzance, two very successful local merchants. In addition to their shipowning activities, they also had interests in fish curing and tin smelting, and the family went on to become merchant bankers and the financiers of many of the subsequent Hain ships. The potential of the ship was doubtless recognised by Edward Hain (II), who commanded her for some years prior to purchase. It was with her that the family gained experience of the deep-sea trades with regular voyages to the Mediterranean with cured fish.

With the delivery of the schooner MYSTERY in 1850, the third Edward Hain, son of Edward (II), became active in the business. Like his father, he was also a master mariner and was to command a number of their vessels. Business prospered, albeit on a small scale, and the financial interest of the Bolithos became more apparent. In addition to the carriage of cured fish to the Mediterranean, returning with Greek and Turkish dried fruit, Hains also entered the West Indies sugar and Brazilian coffee trades.

December 1851 saw the birth of the fourth Edward Hain, followed shortly afterwards by the death of his great grandfather, Edward (I). The succeeding years saw little expansion of the fleet, with never more than three vessels in service at any one time. By now, the fleet was trading even further afield, and in 1862 the brigantine EMILY sailed from Wales on a voyage of 15 months duration which was to include visits to ports in Spain, Canada, Brazil, France, Holland and Ireland. Her cargoes included coal, salt, fish, sugar, oil cake, bran and oats.

GLYNN

P&O Archives

At the time of the death of Edward Hain (II) in February 1866, the fleet consisted of two brigantines GLYNN and EMILY, with a third, MARGARET HAIN (named after the wife of Edward Hain (II)) under construction at Rye. Shareholdings in the vessels were largely divided between the family who owned the major part, and Thomas Bolitho the banker.

After an education in various private schools in St. Ives, Edward Hain (IV) was sent to the local branch of Bolitho's Bank for a training in accountancy and book-keeping. Unlike his father and grandfather, he showed no interest in going to sea and it was recognised that his talents could best be employed in management. After two years at the bank, he moved on to a tea merchant's office in London to gain knowledge of current commercial practice. The combination of the bank training and the time spent in London was to have a profound influence on the development of the company. Upon his return to St. Ives in 1878 he presented his father with an ultimatum — either the company purchase steamships or he would resign.

The year previously, the Hains had taken delivery of their first and only iron barquentine, the T.S.B., a name derived from the initials of Thomas Simon Bolitho. The transition from wood to iron had been a significant development for them and the advance to steamships of more than four times the size must have seemed inconceivable. Although the compound expansion reciprocating engine had been introduced in 1860, steam tramps were still regarded as slow and unreliable. The average steamer rarely exceeded $8\frac{1}{2}$ knots, whereas some of the ocean-going sailing ships could exceed 17 knots in favourable conditions. Edward was convinced that greater profits were to be gained from steam and that the days of sail were numbered. Not the least of his father's worries was the cost, estimated to be some £18,000, and how the vessel was to be financed.

Young Edward was confident that the money could be borrowed from Bolithos Bank and it was eventually agreed to order one steamer if sufficient shareholders could be found who were willing to invest their money. The Bolithos were approached and took no time in deciding to support the venture by standing in with the money until a shareholding could be formed, and in agreeing to take shares themselves. Having secured financial support, young Edward visited the yard of John Readhead and Co. at South Shields, where a lasting relationship with the shipbuilders was formed. The first steamer was ordered and Readheads went on to build 73 more during Edward's lifetime; in fact he never had dealings with any other yard. A total of 87 ships were eventually delivered by Readheads to the company, one of the most outstanding owner/builder associations in British shipbuilding history.

In recognition of the support provided by the Bolithos, the first steamer was named TREWIDDEN after the Bolitho estate outside Penzance. She was launched by the daughter of John Readhead on 26th November 1878 and ran trials off South Shields in January 1879. The contract price was £18,000 which was funded by the issue of 64 shares of £285. The shareholdings in this and subsequent early steamers were for the most part held by members of the Hain and Bolitho families, plus a large number of small investors from St. Ives and neighbouring villages. There seemed to be no shortage of potential investors and an examination of early lists shows master mariners, farmers, mine agents, and even local shopkeepers. This was to be the pattern of shareholding until the formation of the limited liability company in 1901. Very often the same shareholders, such as the Hayle ship chandler Biggleston Spray and the St. Ives draper Richard Permewan purchased one or two shares in each successive ship. If funds were not readily available, the Bolitho Bank was always ready to advance the money at a suitable rate of interest. In succeeding years the variety of shareholders increased to include merchants and agents in Smyrna and the Black Sea ports, which was indicative of the Black Sea grain trade in which the ships were engaged in those early days.

TREVANION (I) at Weymouth in October 1909, discharging a cargo of barley from the Sea of Azov   K. Ingram Collection

After 1883 a number of ships were registered to conform with the Companies' Acts of 1862 to 1880. This resulted in the formation of single ship companies with limited liability and a share issue considerably in excess of the former sixty-fourth system. Edward Hain (III) and Edward Hain (IV) were appointed sole directors of all the single ship companies and designated

TREGURNO (I) loading coal at Swansea   *P&O Archives*

managers of the ships. For this they received $2\frac{1}{2}$% on the gross earnings of each steamer plus travelling and other expenses incurred. By 1901 the fleet had increased spectacularly to 22 steamers with an estimated value of £500,000. It was then decided to amalgamate the single ship companies into one limited liability company. On 16th September 1901 The Hain Steamship Company Limited was registered with a capital of £500,000 in £10 shares.

The steady development of his shipping business did little to hinder Edward's interest in politics. In 1883 he had been elected a member of the St. Ives Town Council, and the following year he was chosen as mayor. He undertook his duties conscientiously and was, as a result, re-elected to that office in 1885 and 1886. He was later elected for further terms in 1889, 1895 and 1899. He served as a councillor and alderman for 20 years, and was also a county councillor for Cornwall for 15 years. In 1885 he was placed on the Commission of Peace for St. Ives and in 1889 on the list of County Justices. With such a background it was hardly surprising that he decided to stand for Parliament, and in 1900 he was elected unopposed as Member for the St. Ives constituency. The seat had become vacant following the retirement of Thomas Bedford Bolitho. Edward Hain (IV) held the seat as a Liberal-Unionist until 1906, when increasing business pressures forced his resignation. Public office still attracted him however, and in 1912 he was appointed High Sheriff for Cornwall. His standing in shipping circles was by now considerable, and in 1910 he was elected President of the Chamber of Shipping. This was followed in 1912 by a knighthood for services to British shipping.

His fleet continued to expand at a rapid rate following the incorporation in 1901, and by 1913 numbered 36 ships. In addition, there were a further five on order at Readheads. The rapid expansion prompted one shareholder to ask at an Annual General Meeting "Good God, where is the money coming from?" to which Sir Edward nonchalantly replied "That's just what we want to know!"

He had good reason to be casual with his reply, for the expansion of the fleet had been completely financed out of revenue without making any fresh issue of capital. As noted earlier, all the new steamers were coming from Readheads on Tyneside, who in 1907 had launched their 50th for the company — the

TREVINCE (I) in the pontoon dock at Penarth   *K. Ingram Collection*

TREVINCE. At her launching, Edward Hain (IV) observed that one ship out of every five built by Readheads since 1878 had been built for his company, and he had signed all 50 contracts.

The company entered the 1914 war in a strong financial position and with a respectable fleet. Unfortunately two steamers TREGLISSON 4265/12 and TREVIDER 4260/13 were berthed in German ports at the outbreak and were both detained for the duration. They were declared total losses in 1915 by the North of England Protection and Indemnity Association, and the company was paid £50,000 for each vessel in compensation. Both were returned to the United Kingdom at the cessation of hostilities, and the company exercised its option to repossess them. The company also lost the services of TREVORIAN 4144/11, which was trapped in the Black Sea and came under Russian control. Like the other two she survived the war, but was wrecked in 1919 on her return voyage from Novorossisk. A further 18 vessels were lost by enemy action and 100 lives were lost.

Sir Edward suffered a severe blow in 1915 when his only son Edward (V) was killed at Gallipoli during the Dardanelles campaign. He had been serving as a captain with the Cornish Squadron of the Royal 1st Devon Yeomanry. Edward (V) had been training in the family business for a number of years and his father never fully recovered from his loss. In June 1917, Sir Edward suffered a severe breakdown during a German air-raid on London, and returned to Cornwall to convalesce. On 20th September 1917 he died at his home Treloyhan, St. Ives, and the news stunned the shipping world. Lord Inchcape of the P&O Steam Navigation Company fully appreciated the value of the fleet, and on 27th October 1917 an offer to purchase was made. The fleet, which at this time numbered 23 vessels, was valued at £2,000,000 and cash assets were held of a similar value. The P&O therefore offered £80 per share, valuing the total shareholding of 49,957 shares at £3,996,560. In addition, they agreed to pay £400,000 compensation to the retiring partners in Edward Hain and Son. The company was therefore acquired for £4,396,560. It is still remembered in St. Ives how Lord Inchcape and Robert Sawle Read embarked

11

Dazzle-painting the funnel of **TREGARTHEN (II)** at Torrevieja, Spain, early in 1918

K. Ingram Collection

on the local fishing boat MOPPET and sailed into the Bay, where all contracts were signed. Immediately upon acquisition, P&O sold 50% of their shareholding to their subsidiary British India Steam Navigation Co. Ltd. and these two companies thereafter remained the sole shareholders.

It was Lord Inchcape's intention from the outset to keep Hain as a separate entity within the group and management of the fleet was to remain firmly in the hands of the Hain directors with P&O exerting overall control. One of the first consequences of the takeover, was an increase in the importance of the London office. The company had long had a presence in the capital, the first office being opened in 1887 in partnership with Robert Sawle Read, an accountant from St. Ives. It was not too long before the directors were moved to London, and the St. Ives office was left to deal with staffing matters. In addition to London and St. Ives, the company employed a considerable staff at Cardiff, where an office had been opened as early as 1881. This operation was run by another partner, Richard Andrews Foster, and he was responsible for the chartering of ships for outward coal cargoes, bunkering, storing, dry-docking and repairing. In later years a small engineering company, Roath Engineering Co. Ltd. was established there.

Having satisfactorily acquired control of Hain, P&O next made moves to acquire the long established London shipowner Mercantile Steam Ship Co. Ltd. Mercantile had grown from the activities of the brothers John and Charles Dunkerly, who purchased their first vessel NILE in 1865. The company prospered, and at the outbreak of war in 1914 they were running a fleet of some 14 tramps, with two further vessels under construction.

However, as a result of heavy war losses and poor prospects for the future, the directors made it known that the company was available for disposal. The P&O was once again interested and late in 1917, Hain acquired the majority of shares in the company at a cost of £1,484,944. The remaining shares were purchased in the years 1922 and 1923, and by 31st March 1923, the whole of the share capital was held by Hain.

For the first few years after 1917 the Mercantile fleet continued to trade as before, with Hain acting as managers. No new vessels were ordered, although in 1921 Hain transferred to Mercantile the contract for one of the ships they had under construction at Readheads. This ship was to be completed in July 1922 as the MIN. However, it soon became apparent to the P&O Board that there was little to be gained in running two separate companies in the tramping trades. Therefore on 21st June 1923 the Mercantile Board resolved to put the company into voluntary liquidation and transfer the fleet assets to Hain. Although the Mercantile steamers were promptly repainted in Hain colours, their traditional names were retained, and did in fact last until 1936. Then, at a board meeting in September of that year, it was finally resolved to preserve the uniformity of the fleet names. As a result, the former Mercantile steamers plus NIMODA and NOHATA of 1928, were all given "manufactured" Cornish names with the prefix "TRE".

No sooner had the acquisition of Mercantile been completed than the directors embarked upon further financial manoeuvrings. Once again the influence of Inchcape and the P&O were much in evidence. This time their efforts were directed towards a number of companies formerly controlled by the veteran shipowner Frank C. Strick. His fleet and business had been sold to Lord Inchcape's personal company, Gray, Dawes and Co. after the War, and in May 1923 they offered it to P&O and it was decided that Hain should purchase the whole of the share capital four Strick companies — Strick Line (1923) Ltd., The Shahristan Steamship Co. Ltd., The Turkistan Steamship Co. Ltd. and The Serbistan Steamship Co. Ltd. The four companies were purchased for £573,468, a loan being arranged to cover the cost. The purchase was almost certainly undertaken for the financial benefit of the P&O since the companies were engaged almost exclusively in the Arabian Gulf liner trades, and would seem totally incompatible with Hain's existing business.

In 1928, in spite of his advancing years (he was by now 79) Frank Strick approached Inchcape and expressed an interest in returning to the Gulf trade. After selling his fleet and business to Inchcape in 1920 he had registered the London, Paris and Marseilles Steamship Co. Ltd. and it was through this company that he intended restoring his interest. The purchase of a 49% minority shareholding was negotiated by Frank Strick in Strick Line (1923) Ltd. and The Shahristan Steamship Co. Ltd. for £236,228. The Turkistan Steamship Co. Ltd. and The Serbistan Steamship Co. Ltd. were then to be liquidated. Hain retained the controlling interest in the two trading companies until September 1935, when they were sold to the P&O for £210,000. P&O ultimately acquired the Strick minorities in 1972.

The Hain company had suffered heavily in the war, losing 18 vessels as a result of enemy action and three by marine causes. Fortunately, two which had been detained in German ports, TREGLISSON and TREVIDER, were returned in 1919 and quickly put back into service. New vessels had been delivered from Readheads throughout the war, but at a rate far below the level of losses. Further orders were placed with the yard when hostilities ceased, but under the new ownership, the dependence on this one yard was about to change. Under the guidance of Lord Inchcape, negotiations were commenced for the purchase of 16 wartime standard ships. These were of various types and from a number of different yards, as follows:

A-type cargo carriers	B-type cargo carriers	H-type small cargo carrier
WAR ACONITE	WAR BULLDOG	WAR QUINCE
WAR JONQUIL	WAR GANNET	
WAR LAUREL	WAR MALLARD	Z-type heavy oiler
WAR LILAC	WAR PLOVER	
WAR LILY	WAR QUAIL	WAR AIRMAN
WAR PALM	WAR STAG	
WAR PAMPAS		
WAR PICOTEE		

In addition, the company purchased seven ex-German prizes from The Shipping Controller at a total cost of £1,027,000. These were not entirely suitable for their use and five were soon transferred to the Federal Steam Navigation Co. Ltd., another company controlled by P&O A further vessel, TREVESSA, was soon lost, and only TRELEVAN remained in the fleet.

The influence of P&O over the company increased during the following years and Hain were asked to manage and crew a number of P&O cargo liners on their Eastern services. It was not long before they began to order vessels specifically for use on P&O routes and the first of these, NIMODA and NOHATA, were launched late in 1927. This order was followed by one for four $14\frac{1}{2}$ knot cargo liners, launched as BANGALORE, BURDWAN, BEHAR and BHUTAN. These latter vessels were permanently employed on P&O services, although registered under Hain Steamship and manned, stored, maintained and repaired by them. All were to become war losses, but in May 1941 a further vessel in the series was ordered from Barclay, Curle, at a cost of £395,000. This, the second BEHAR, only lasted eight months before she was sunk in the Pacific by a Japanese cruiser. A further two vessels for P&O service were ordered, SOMALI and SOUDAN, but although the former was launched for Hain, both were sold to P&O before completion.

14

TREWIDDEN (III), TRECARNE (I), TREVORIAN (III) and TREFUSIS (II)
laid up in the River Fal in the 1930s   *K. Ingram Collection*

The income from the vessels on charter to P&O undoubtedly helped the company over the lean years of the 1930s. In common with most shipowners, much of their fleet was laid up for long periods, the company favouring the River Fal in Cornwall. In 1930 as many as 15 of their vessels were idle in a stretch of the river between Woodbury and Tolverne known locally as Hain's Alley or Reach. They used this location for many years, the last time being in 1963 when TREMAYNE was laid up there for a brief period. During these years of recession the income earned was pitifully low and in many cases failed to cover running costs. It is however a tribute to the expertise of the Head Office staff that even in the blackest years the fleet usually made a profit on voyages, albeit at times a very small one. In the year ending March 1934, the profit on voyages for a fleet of 34 vessels after charging the cost of laying up tonnage, was a mere £33,029. This compares with £656,422 in the greatly improved year ending March 1938.

TREFUSIS (II) laid up in the River Fal on 8th July 1931   *John G. Callis*

Despite the poor prospects for the forseeable future, a contract was signed on 11th September 1935 with Lithgows Ltd., Port Glasgow, for two new vessels of 5,200 gross tons. The cost was to be £92,595 each, payable one fifth on laying of the keel, one fifth on completion of framing, one fifth on completion of plating, one fifth on launching and one fifth on delivery. The

BUILDING THE TREVALGAN 1936-1937

Photographs: Courtesy of The Hain Room, St. Ives Museum

Keel laid, 2nd September 1936

The stern framing

Floors erected, 21st November 1936

16

contract was completed as TREWELLARD and TREGARTHEN in July and September 1936 respectively. It was soon followed by another with the same yard for a further two vessels of identical dimensions. TREVALGAN and TREVANION, built at a cost of £110,975 each, were to be the first motorships in the fleet.

Forepeak bulkhead completed, 27th January 1937

Plating completed, 31st March 1937

The bow section, partly plated, 9th March 1937

TREVALGAN in tow for pre-delivery dry-docking, 27th August 1937

Captain's cabin, **TREVALGAN**

At the outbreak of the Second World War, the fleet numbered 24 vessels with a further three on order. The latter had all been ordered from Clydeside yards in April 1939 at a cost of approximately £156,000 each. It was not long before the company suffered its first loss, TREVANION of 1937. She fell victim to the German pocket battleship ADMIRAL GRAF SPEE when five days out from Cape Town and her crew were taken prisoner. After an interval of several months there were further losses and their frequency increased as the war progressed. The level of losses was in fact so high that all of the vessels in commission in 1939 were eventually lost plus two of those on order. In part, their place was taken by Ministry of War Transport tonnage allocated to the company for management, a total of 30 such vessels being entrusted to them.

It had always been company policy to replace losses with newbuildings, but the rapid rate of loss during the war made this impracticable. Orders were placed for new tonnage, especially in 1942, but yard space was at a premium. As a result, the company entered into negotiations with the London shipowner J. and C. Harrison for the purchase of four motorships, all less than two years old. As a result, contracts were signed on 24th January 1944 for the purchase of HARLESDEN 7273/43, HARPAGUS 7271/42, HARPALYCE 7269/42 and HARDINGHAM 7269/42. Because of Ministry commitments, delivery of HARPALYCE and HARDINGHAM was considerably delayed as can be seen from the accompanying table. In addition, another Doxford motorship, REGISTAN 7368/44, was purchased from Strick Line.

Vessel	Contract Signed	Delivered	Cost
HARLESDEN	24.1.1944	18. 2.1944	£234,450
HARPAGUS	24.1.1944	16. 5.1944	£232,450
HARPALYCE	24.1.1944	30.11.1944	£231,450
HARDINGHAM	24.1.1944	13.12.1944	£229,450
REGISTAN	2.7.1945	9. 7.1945	£233,000

At the cessation of hostilities the company was left with a fleet of 11 vessels, all motorships. Although new tonnage was ordered, the opportunity was taken to bid for a number of "Empire" ships under the Ministry of Transport's Ship Disposal Scheme. Bids were placed for a total of six vessels, but only that for EMPIRE TILBURY at £250,000 was successful. She entered the fleet in March 1946 as TREVEAN. Doxford at Sunderland had earlier been given an order for a further four motorships of the TREWIDDEN type at an estimated price of £258,000 each. Within three months of the order it was decided to increase their engine size from three to four cylinders at an additional cost of £15,640 per ship. A backward step was taken in December 1946 when two steamships were ordered. This was the first order to be placed at the Readhead yard for 24 years, and a price of £310,000 each was agreed. A further steamship was ordered from William Hamilton early in 1948, but all three were soon to prove uneconomic and were disposed of to Pakistani owners within ten years of delivery.

The launch on 16th February 1949 of **TREGENNA (V)**, the first of the Readhead steamships ordered in December 1946
K. Ingram Collection

Although the vessels permanently engaged on P&O services had all been lost in the war, tonnage was still chartered to that company when required. Late in 1950 it was agreed to sell three motorships to the P&O for approximately £112,000 each. The value had been written down for tax purposes and there was an agreement allowing Hain to repurchase them at a later date. Crewing and management was to remain in the hands of Hain. Consequently early in 1951 TRESILLIAN 7368/44, TREVOSE 7354/44 and TREVETHOE 7355/44 were all registered under the ownership of The Peninsular and Oriental Steam Navigation Company. In 1956 a further four motorships were transferred — TREWORLAS 7271/42, TREVELYAN 7292/43, TREWELLARD 7269/42 and TREVEAN 7312/45. All were returned in 1958 with the exception of TRESILLIAN which had been lost in the North Atlantic in November 1954.

During 1957 Hain finalised plans for the closure of Roath Engineering Co. Ltd., their Cardiff subsidiary. This company had been formed in 1925 in association with R. & H. Green and Silley Weir, another P&O company, to carry out work afloat on their vessels. At that time Hain were regular users of the South Wales ports, and are reputed to have boasted that there was never a time when there was not a white "H" in the Bristol Channel. Many of their outward cargoes were fixed on the Cardiff Exchange and the office of Foster, Hain and Read at Salvage Buildings, Cardiff, was particularly busy. Since most of the fleet was using the port it was considered appropriate for the company to undertake their own minor repairs there. Drydocking and underwater work was however undertaken by outside contractors.

TREVETHOE (IV) undergoing voyage repairs in Roath Dock, Cardiff
Welsh Industrial & Maritime Museum

The works were located in Roath Dock, Cardiff, and consisted of a large machine shop, boiler shop, blacksmith's and coppersmith's shops. Until the War, Roath worked almost exclusively on Hain vessels, and little effort was made to secure outside contracts. With the outbreak of war things changed and the company started working for the Admiralty, especially on frigate overhauls. This work continued after the cessation of hostilities and was supplemented by considerable outside commercial work. A notable contract was the conversion of the Flower class corvette HYDRANGEA into the merchant HYDRALOCK. Hain vessels now rarely loaded coal in the port, but Roath was kept busy with major engine repairs on their vessels. All of the motorships were fitted with Doxford engines which after a few years gave considerable trouble on account of pitting. It was necessary to strip down the engines, remetal the bearings and machine the journals. This constituted a major overhaul and was carried out on virtually the entire fleet. The lifeboats for many of the newbuildings were also constructed by Roath. However, developments around the site, and out-dated machinery, meant that the days of the company were limited, and in February 1957 the decision was taken to close down. Trading ceased on 4th February 1957 and all plant and stock was sold to C. H. Bailey Ltd.

Company profits throughout the early 1950s had been maintained at satisfactory levels and the fleet was fully employed. They were further helped in 1956 by the Suez crisis which provided a sudden and unexpected boost to freight rates. The financial year ending September 1957 saw profits of £1,094,678, an increase of almost 60% on the previous year. Confident of an improving freight market, a new construction programme was embarked upon, and by March 1957 seven new vessels had been ordered. Delivery was scheduled over the period 1957 to 1961 and the first to be completed TREMEADOW, was handed over to the company by William Hamilton and Co. Ltd. at Princes Pier, Greenock on 29th January 1958. She was immediately chartered to Federal Steam Navigation Co. Ltd. of London for five years, proof that tonnage now being built for the fleet was more than suited for service on the liner trades.

Unfortunately in 1957 the freight market collapsed and by June 1958 the Board were concerned about the volume of tonnage on order. Negotiations were commenced with William Hamilton and John Readhead in an attempt to cancel or defer their newbuildings numbered 523 (Hamilton) and 604 and 609 (Readhead). Work on numbers 523 and 604 was found to be so advanced that cancellation or even deferral would cause serious problems. However an agreement was reached with Readhead to defer Yard No. 609 indefinitely for ultimate completion at a time satisfactory to Hain. At that time a completion date of 1963/64 was being considered. In addition to the steps taken above, the company started to book lay up berths, anticipating that a considerable proportion of the fleet would soon be without employment. The first two

TREGOTHNAN (II) in London Docks   *St. Ives Museum*

vessels, the steamships TREGOTHNAN and TREGENNA, were laid up at Milford Haven on 22nd May and 6th June 1958 respectively.

As freight rates fell ever lower efforts were made to dispose of some of the older units in the fleet. TREVETHOE of 1944 was the first to go, sold for

£143,000 to Panamanian owners after a short period of lay up in the River Fal. By late 1958 most of the fleet was trading at a loss and a deficit for the year of over £300,000 was envisaged. Finances did not deteriorate to this extent however and the bottom was reached during the year ending September 1960 when the profit on voyages was only £32,704. Already signs of a slight improvement were in evidence and negotiations were recommenced with Readheads for the completion of Yard No. 609. The vessel, which had been ordered on 23rd November 1956, was restarted on 8th March 1960 as a fixed value contract priced at £1,100,000 with delivery scheduled for September 1961. She was to be completed as TREFUSIS. During 1960 what were to be the final vessels in the Hain fleet were ordered. Two of these orders went to the Readhead yard at South Shields and marked the end of Hain's very long association with that builder. The third TRENEGLOS went to William Hamilton, and although launched for Hain, she was on completion registered in the ownership of another P&O subsidiary, the New Zealand Shipping Co. Ltd.

TRENEGLOS (V)   *Airfoto, Malacca*

Freight rates remained at very low levels throughout the early 1960s and prompted the main P&O Board to undertake a detailed review of all their shipping operations. The conclusion was reached that there was not much of a future for general tramp shipping under the British flag. As such vessels were amongst the cheapest and simplest to operate, it was foreseen that the newly developing nations would be anxious to acquire them and so create considerable competition. In addition, the bulk carrier was seizing much of the traditional tramp business. As a first step, the fleet was amalgamated for operational purposes with that of fellow P&O subsidiary James Nourse Ltd. of London. A new management company Hain-Nourse Management Ltd. was registered on 29th January 1964 and became responsible for the operation of the Hain and Nourse fleets. On 1st July 1964 all shore and seagoing staff were transferred to the employment of that company. Further restructuring took place in 1965 when the fleet and trades of Nourse were finally transferred to Hain. In consequence, The Hain Steamship Co. Ltd. was renamed Hain-Nourse Ltd. on 1st October 1965. In addition to the Nourse fleet, that of the

Asiatic Steam Navigation Co. Ltd. was also acquired. The new company also took over the management of two bulk carriers, ATHERSTONE and BUCCLEUCH, which were registered with other group companies. Further bulk carriers were to follow in 1966.

BUCCLEUCH   *F. R. Sherlock*

The developments envisaged in the aforementioned P&O review became reality in the latter years of the decade. Competition from the developing nations coupled with the rapid growth of free flag fleets made further reorganisation inevitable. In the matter of a few years the container had revolutionised the liner trades and the days of the large liner fleets were numbered. In common with most other British operators, P&O elected to join one of the new consortia being formed in order to share the high cost of container ships and equipment. They therefore became a significant shareholder in Overseas Containers Ltd., and were in 1986 to acquire complete control of the company.

The reorganisation of the early 1960s (which included combining P&O and Orient passenger operations and setting up a specialist tanker company, Trident Tankers Ltd., as well as the Hain-Nourse merger) now led to the total reorganisation of the P&O Group along lines suggested by management consultants McKinsey and Co. early in 1971. The steady introduction of the new container ships meant a surplus of general cargo ships and reorganisation into "operating divisions" was commenced. Four principal shipping divisions were formed, these being:-

1) P&O Bulk Shipping Division. This was to include the bulk carriers formerly managed by Hain-Nourse Ltd., the tankers and gas carriers of Trident Tankers Ltd. plus bulk shipping registered under other P&O subsidiaries.

2) P&O General Cargo Division. In time this was to include all general cargo vessels in the subsidiary fleets, and was to include the last of the former Hain TRE-boats.

3) European and Air Transport. Its Short Sea Shipping sector included the former Coast Lines and General Steam fleets and similar vessels.

4) P&O Passenger Division. To include the passenger and cruise liners.

Over the next few years all the former Hain-Nourse fleet was to be registered in the ownership of the P&O Steam Navigation Company, and for a time the former owning company lay dormant. It was to be briefly revived in 1975 when the new 4,000 ton ro/ro ships BISON and BUFFALO were

BUFFALO   *W. J. Harvey*

introduced. However the name no longer seemed appropriate and was soon changed to P&O Ferries Ltd., and as such still exists today, owning ships employed on services between Scotland and Orkney and Shetland.

So disappeared one of the great names of British tramp shipping, almost 100 years after the introduction of their first steamship TREWIDDEN. It is perhaps fitting that when the company identity was finally lost in 1972, there was still a TREWIDDEN in the fleet. The fifth vessel of that name, she was to be sold before she could be given one of the P&O "STRATH" names, and therefore never lost her Hain identity whilst under the British flag.

FLEET LIST NOTES

The notation (I), (II) after a ship's name indicates that she is the first, the second etc. ship of that name in the fleet. The dates following the name are those of entering and leaving the fleet, or coming under and leaving the management of the company. The histories are in chronological order according to acquisition (where known) or to the date of launch for newly built ships.

On the first line is given the ship's Official Number (O.N.) in the British Registry, followed by her tonnages (g) and net (n). Dimensions given are registered length x beam x depth in feet and tenths for ships numbered S1-S12, 1-144, A1-A10, MS1-MS4, M1-M30 and B1-B10. The dimensions given for ships numbered 145-153, HN1-HN7 and B11-B17 are the overall length x beam x draught at summer deadweight in feet and inches. In addition, the overall length (o.l.) has been given for some of the earlier ships where shown in the Register. The notation B.B. indicates that the overall length is inclusive of the ship's bulbous bow

On the second line is given the type and make of engine and the name of the engine builders except ships built by Wm. Doxford and fitted with Doxford diesels. In these cases the statement is limited to ". . . oil engine by the shipbuilder". T.3-cyl. denotes triple expansion three cylinder steam engines, C.2-cyl. denotes compound two cylinder steam engines, Q.4-cyl. denotes quadruple expansion four cylinder steam engines and for motor vessels the number of cylinders is given and whether they are two stroke cycle (2.S.C.), single acting (S.A.) or (D.A.) double acting.

The ships' histories are corrected up to July 1986.

FLEET LIST
SAILING SHIPS

S1.   DASHER (1816 — 1841) Fishing lugger.
17   registered tons. 39.0 × 10.8 × 6.1 feet.
1816: Launched at St. Ives for Edward Hain, Michael Welch and Matthew Daniel. *2.12.1825:* Transferred to Edward Hain and Michael Welch. *3.3.1841:* Sold to James Paynter, St. Ives. *13.3.1865:* Registry closed and vessel broken up.

S2.   CAMILLA (1838 — 1851) Schooner.
135g, 114n. 71.0 × 18.2 × 11.1 feet.
1826: Launched by Hill, Plymouth, for Phillips. *1828:* Sold to Douglas. *1830:* Sold to Bolitho and Co., Penzance. *17.2.1838:* Purchased by Edward Hain and Co. *9.1851:* When entering Bute Docks, Cardiff, jammed against the schooner VENUS 123/27 and sank. Refloated on the next tide, but found to be beyond economical repair and sold to London shipbreakers.

S3.   MYSTERY (1850 — 1860) Schooner.
O.N. 8458. 114n. 75.2 × 17.6 × 11.1 feet.
21.11.1850: Launched by Hoad Brothers, Rye, for Hain and Son. *20.4.1860:* Driven ashore on Porthgwidden Beach, Cornwall, when on passage from Swansea to Smyrna. She was declared a total loss, stripped of her cargo and fittings and broken up.

S4.   BOHEMIAN GIRL (1852 — 1860) Schooner.
O.N. 19349. 175g. 157n. 76.0 × 18.8 × 11.1 feet.
1843: Launched by White, Waterford, for Ogilby and Co., London. *1849:* Sold to Newson and Co., London. *15.3.1852:* Purchased by Edward Hain. *13.11.1859:* In collision with an unidentified brig off the Portuguese coast whilst on a voyage from Genoa and Gallipoli to Hull with a cargo of oil. She was abandoned by her crew, but later taken in tow to Corunna where *10.1860* she was sold to meet salvage expenses to Fox, Sons and Co., Plymouth. *1874:* Sold to Short and Co., Plymouth. *1875:* Owners restyled Marshall and Short. *1887:* Sold to Stuart McGiffen, Carrickfergus. *1890:* Sold to Frederic Lowes, Swansea. *3.1893:* Sold to Peter Garriock, Lerwick. *27.10.1899:* Sailed from Sunderland for Wick with a cargo of coal. Wreckage was subsequently washed ashore on the island of Whalsay, but no subsequent news of the vessel was received.

GLYNN aground off Lelant, 11th September 1885   *Royal Institute of Cornwall*

S5.   GLYNN (1857 — 1882) Brigantine.
O.N. 17567. 138n. 92.0 × 21.3 × 12.1 feet.
22.7.1857: Launched by Hoad Brothers, Rye, for Edward Hain. *1864:* Registered under J. Hain and Co. *1875:* Returned to Edward Hain. *1882:* Sold to W. Walles, Cardiff. *11.9.1885:* Wrecked in the Lelant Estuary when on passage from Cardiff to Cherbourg with a cargo of coal.

25

S6.   EMILY (1861 — 1882) Brigantine.
O.N. 29590. 161g, 145n. 96.6 × 22.6 × 12.6 feet.
12.3.1861: Launched by Hoad Brothers, Rye, for Edward Hain and Co. *1882:* Sold to William C. Phillips, Port Isaac, Cornwall. *11.6.1888:* Sank in the River Scheldt following a collision with the steamship MANITOBA, 2127/87, when on passage from Teignmouth to Antwerp.

MARGARET HAIN   *P&O Archives*

S7.   MARGARET HAIN (1866 — 1889) Brigantine.
O.N. 52863. 170n. 100.6 × 23.9 × 12.9 feet.
2.1.1866: Launched by Hoad Brothers, Rye, for Edward Hain and Co. *27.2.1889:* Wrecked at Saffi.

S8.   ARETHUSA (1868 — 1874) Barque.
O.N. 19358. 220n. 112.2 × 23.1 × 14.0 feet.
8.1.1852: Launched by W. Bayley, Ipswich, for A. Williams, London. *1854:* Sold to William Bolitho, Penzance. *22.7.1868:* Purchased by Edward Hain and Co. *27.4.1874:* Sank following a collision in dense fog with the steamship CINGALESE, 1299/70, off Cape Finisterre, whilst on a voyage from Smyrna to Nantes with a cargo of dried fruit. There were only two survivors.

S9.   A. D. GILBERT (1872 — 1886) Schooner.
O.N. 51313. 177n. 108.0 × 23.5 × 12.5 feet.
10.1865: Launched by Hodge, Truro, for William Hodge, Truro. *7.1872:* Purchased by Edward Hain and Co. *28.10.1886:* Stranded off Chipiona Light, Spain, and became a total loss. *6.11.1886:* The hull was sold at auction and broken up.

S10.   JANIE BANFIELD (1874 — 1875) Topsail schooner.
O.N. 49989. 190 registered tons. 108.8 × 25.1 × 12.6 feet.
10.1866: Launched by Stribley, Padstow, for John Harvey Trevithick, Hayle. *8.11.1866:* Completed. *20.4.1874:* Purchased by Edward Hain. *17.3.1875:* Wrecked on the island of Nicero.

S11.   KESTREL (1875 — 1880) Schooner.
O.N. 65344. 158g, 151n. 102.6 × 22.0 × 11.9 feet.
10.10.1874: Launched by Henry S. Trethowan, Falmouth, for E. Pope, Falmouth. *1875:* Sold to Hall and Co., Bristol. *1875:* Purchased by Edward Hain. *1880:* Sold to J. Munn and Co., Newfoundland and *1892* registered under Robert Stewart Munn. Upon his death, registered under his trustees, John F. Apsey and Alfred G. Smith, who on 14.6.1895 sold the vessel to Robert Ehlers, Bristol. *31.7.1895:* Sold to George Kearon, Arklow, but Canadian registry retained. *1899:* Transferred to John F. Storey, Arklow. *10.1916:* Sold to John William Kingston (John Carter, manager), Poole. *14.3.1918:* Wrecked on the Pipette Rocks, Minquiers, when on a voyage from Fowey to St. Malo with china clay.

S12.   T.S.B. (1877 — 1882) Iron Barquentine.
O.N. 78079. 289g, 276n. 137.4 × 26.2 × 12.5 feet.
29.10.1877: Launched by Harvey and Co., Hayle, for Edward Hain. *1882:* Sold to Thomas C. Guthrie, Glasgow, and renamed PENPONT. *1890:* Sold to James de V. Le Couteur, Germany (Glasgow registry retained). *19.9.1894:* Wrecked 20 miles N. of Rio Grande Bar, when on passage from Rangoon to Rio Janeiro. Her crew was rescued.

FLEET LIST

STEAM AND MOTOR VESSELS

TREWIDDEN   *South Tyneside Museum*

1.   TREWIDDEN (I) (1878 — 1891)
O.N. 67899. 1271g, 824n. 240.0 × 32.1 × 17.9 feet.
C. 2-cyl. by the Shipbuilder.
26.11.1878: Launched by J. Readhead and Co., South Shields (Yard No. 146), for Edward Hain
and Son. *1891:* Sold to Vagliano Bros., Greece, and renamed ADELPHI. *1893:* Sold to G. L. Vatis,
Greece. *27.2.1896:* Wrecked opposite Messina, at Brancalenoe, Calabria.

2.   TREGENNA (I) (1880 — 1892)
O.N. 67900. 1332g, 864n. 245.0 × 32.7 × 18.0 feet.
C. 2-cyl. by the Shipbuilder.
13.1.1880: Launched by J. Readhead and Co., South Shields (Yard No. 156), for Edward Hain
and Son. *16.1.1892:* Sold to David Russell, Alfred Tennant Miller and David Huskie, Leith.
9.2.1892: Registered under The Steamship Tregenna Co. Ltd. (Russell, Miller and Huskie,
managers). *1897:* Sold to Tregenna Steamship Co. Ltd. (Miller and Richards, managers), Glasgow.
29.11.1898: Sold to Steamship Ashgrove Co. Ltd. (Alexander and Arthurs, managers), Glasgow.
7.3.1900: Sold to Robson Brown and Sons Ltd., Sunderland. *1920:* Sold to Soc. Anon. de Gerance
et d'Armement, France, and renamed CAP LA HEVE. *1923:* Sold to Rederi Aktieb. Carrie (G. F.
Persson, manager), Sweden, and renamed CARRIE. *1925:* Sold to Rederi Aktieb. Cecil — same
manager. *1933:* Sold to shipbreakers.

3.   TREVILLEY (I) (1881 — 1895)
O.N. 81672. 1275g, 810n. 245.8 × 32.7 × 18.0 feet.
C. 2-cyl. by the Shipbuilder.
4.1881: Launched by J. Readhead and Co., South Shields (Yard No. 169), for Edward Hain and
Son. *11.5.1881:* Ran trials. *1895:* Sold to B. Repetto, Italy, and renamed MARIQUITA. *1900:* Sold
to W. S. Miller and Co., Glasgow, and renamed TREVILLEY. *28.9.1901:* Sailed from Castro, Spain,
for Glasgow with a cargo of iron ore and disappeared.

4.   TRENEGLOS (I) (1882 — 1883)
O.N. 81673. 1513g, 973n. 249.0 × 36.1 × 17.5 feet.
C. 2-cyl. by the Shipbuilder.
4.2.1882: Launched by J. Readhead and Co., South Shields (Yard No. 178), for Edward Hain and
Son. *30.7.1883:* Wrecked on Bridge Rock, Limerick, whilst on a voyage from Galatz to Limerick.
Salvage was attempted and approximately 700 tons of her cargo of maize was discharged before
the hull broke in two and sank in deep water.

TRELYON as ELSIE   J. Clarkson

5. TRELYON (I) (1882 — 1895)
O.N. 81674. 1428g, 897n. 249.0 × 36.1 × 17.5 feet.
C. 2-cyl. by the Shipbuilder.
12.8.1882: Launched by J. Readhead and Co., South Shields (Yard No. 184), for Edward Hain
and Son. *4.9.1895:* Sold to Cairnlyon S.S. Co. Ltd. (Cairns, Young and Noble, managers),
Newcastle and renamed CAIRNLYON. *1901:* Transferred to Cairnglen S.S. Co. Ltd. (same
managers). *1903:* Managers restyled as Cairns, Noble and Co. *1912:* Sold to Rederiaktieb. Anglos
(A. Johnsson, manager), Sweden, and renamed ELSIE. *1916:* Management transferred to Carl
Norrthon. *1918:* Sold to Rederiaktieb. H. Modin (H. Modin, manager), Sweden. *1920:* Sold to John
Bohman, Sweden. *1923:* Sold to Rederi. Aktieb. Elsie (J. Holmstrom, manager), Sweden. *1935:*
Sold to Rederi Aktieb. Fram (Algot Johansson, manager), Finland. *12.11.1939:* Wrecked off
Terschelling whilst on a voyage from Viipuri to Zaandam with a cargo of timber.

6. TREVOSE (I) (1882 — 1895)
O.N. 81675. 1493g, 941n. 259.5 × 36.0 × 17.5 feet.
C.2-cyl. by the Shipbuilder.
24.10.1882: Launched by J. Readhead and Co., South Shields (Yard No. 187), for Edward Hain
and Son. *1895:* Sold to Fratelli Sanguineti fu G., Italy and renamed ANGELA. *1911:* Sold to Ilva
Soc. Anon. con Sede in Genova, Italy. *1919:* Sold to Lloyd Mediterraneo Societa Italiana di Nav.,
Italy. *1924:* Sold to Gio. Batta Bibolini, Italy and renamed PERTUSOLA. *1951:* Sold to Navigazione
Sardegna S.A., Italy. *1954:* Sold to Cantieri di Portovenere and *17.12.1954* arrived at La Spezia
to be broken up.

TREKIEVE   E. N. Taylor

28

7. TREKIEVE (I) (1883 — 1897)
O.N. 81676. 1489g, 939n. 259.0 × 36.1 × 17.6 feet.
C.2-cyl. by the Shipbuilder.
26.4.1883: Launched by J. Readhead and Co., South Shields (Yard No. 193), for Edward Hain and Son. *31.7.1897:* Wrecked at Connah's Quay whilst on a voyage from Carthagena to Mostyn with a cargo of iron ore. She broke in two and was declared a total loss.

TREVIDER as CAIRNBAHN   *K. O'Donoghue Collection*

8. TREVIDER (I) (1883 — 1898)
O.N. 81677. 1538g, 974n. 259.5 × 36.1 × 17.8 feet.
C.2-cyl. by the Shipbuilder.
29.10.1883: Launched by J. Readhead and Co., South Shields (Yard No. 200), for Edward Hain and Son. *1885:* Transferred to Trevider Steamship Co. Ltd. (Edward Hain and Son, managers). *13.1.1898:* Sold to Gaelic Steamships Ltd. (Cairns, Young and Noble, managers), Newcastle and renamed CAIRNBAHN. *1903:* Managers restyled as Cairns, Noble and Co. *1913:* Transferred to Cairn Line of Steamships Ltd. (same managers). *1913:* Sold to Rederi Aktieb. Hebe (C. W. von Liewen, manager), Sweden and renamed IGOR. *1917:* Sold to Rederi Aktieb. Igor (L. Norstrom, manager), Sweden. *1918:* Sold to Aktieb. Svenska Amerika Mexico Line (Dan Brostrom, manager), Sweden. *17.9.1918:* Foundered about 10 miles S. of Longstone Light whilst on a voyage from Gothenburg to Hull with a cargo of timber and woodpulp.

9. TRELOSKE (I) (1884 — 1897)
O.N. 81678. 1548g, 980n. 259.0 × 36.1 × 17.6 feet.
C.2-cyl. by the Shipbuilder.
28.2.1884: Launched by J. Readhead and Co., South Shields (Yard No. 205), for Edward Hain and Son. *1889:* Transferred to Treloske Steamship Co. Ltd. *20.12.1897:* Sold to G. P. Cutting and Co., South Shields and *1898* renamed PEARL. *1911:* Sold to Akties. Tordenvore (Lundegaard & Stray, managers), Norway and renamed TORDENVORE. *9.6.1917:* Torpedoed and sunk by the German submarine UC.53, S.W. of Cape Finisterre in a position 42.30 N, 09.08 W.

10. TREVELLOE (1884 — 1894)
O.N. 81679. 1646g, 1062n. 259.5 × 36.2 × 17.6 feet.
C.2-cyl. by the Shipbuilder.
3.1884: Launched by J. Readhead and Co., South Shields (Yard No. 206), for Edward Hain and Son. *1889:* Transferred to Trevelloe Steamship Co. Ltd. (Edward Hain and Son, managers). *9.1.1894:* Stranded in heavy weather at the entrance to the harbour at Sulina, whilst on a voyage from Cardiff to Sulina with a cargo of coal. Declared a constructive total loss, she was eventually refloated 1.6.1894 and towed into port. *1.7.1894:* Sold for £5,300 to Theophilatos Bros., Greece and renamed ODYSSEUS. *1897:* Sold to F. Carnevali, Italy and renamed ODISSEO. *1897:* Renamed UMBRIA. *1899:* Sold to Sociedad Hullera Espanola, Spain and renamed HULLERA ESPANOLA. *4.1.1902:* Sank 100 miles S. of Cape Finisterre following a collision with the British steamship ALFONSO 1325/78, whilst on a voyage from Aviles to Barcelona with a cargo of coal.

11. TRENEGLOS (II) (1885 — 1905)
O.N. 91342. 1559g, 992n. 259.0 × 36.2 × 17.7 feet.
C.2-cyl. by the Shipbuilder.
3.1885: Launched by J. Readhead and Co., South Shields (Yard No. 213), for Edward Hain and Son. *1901:* Transferred to The Hain Steamship Co. Ltd. *27.9.1905:* Sold for £8,000 to Rederiaktieb. Kärnan (B. Ingelsson, manager), Sweden and renamed NORMA. *26.3.1917:* Torpedoed and sunk by the German submarine U.69 in the English Channel, 8 miles S.E. of Ile de la Vierge, whilst on a voyage from Dakar to Dunkirk.

12. TREVEAN (I) (1885 — 1899)
O.N. 91343. 1567g, 999n. 259.0 × 36.1 × 17.8 feet.
C.2-cyl. by the Shipbuilder.
17.4.1885: Launched by J. Readhead and Co., South Shields (Yard No. 214), for Edward Hain and Son. *14.11.1899:* Wrecked near St. Nazaire whilst on a voyage from Cardiff to St. Nazaire with a cargo of coal. Much of the cargo was discharged into lighters.

TREMAYNE   *W.S.P.L.*

13. TREMAYNE (I) (1886 — 1905)
O.N. 91344. 1578g, 997n. 259.0 × 36.0 × 17.9 feet.
C.2-cyl. by the Shipbuilder.
17.6.1886: Launched by J. Readhead and Co., South Shields (Yard No. 222), for Edward Hain and Son. *1901:* Transferred to The Hain Steamship Co. Ltd. *18.4.1905:* Sold for £8,250 to Rederiaktieb. Helios (J. Pettersson, manager), Sweden and renamed HELIOS. *1914:* Sold to Rederiaktieb. Polaris (same managers), Sweden. *1916:* Sold to Rederiaktieb. Helios (R. Gohle, manager), Sweden. *1922:* Sold to Rederiaktieb. Nordsjöen i Helsingborg (A. T. Jonasson, manager), Sweden. *1931:* Management transferred to M. Jonasson. *1936:* Sold to Rederi Aktieb. Helny (A. Abrahamsson, manager), Finland and renamed HELNY. *1942:* Sold to Rederi Aktieb. Eystrasalt (E. Dunér, manager), Sweden and renamed FRIGG. *28.4.1944:* Sank off Kiel after striking a wreck whilst on a voyage from Emden to Sundsvall with a cargo of coke.

TRELAWNY   *W.S.S.-Brownell Collection*

30

14.   TRELAWNY (I) (1888 — 1905)
O.N. 91345. 1658g, 1047n. 259.0 × 36.0 × 17.9 feet.
T.3-cyl. by the Shipbuilder.
30.1.1888: Launched by J. Readhead and Co., South Shields (Yard No. 232), for Edward Hain and Son. *5.3.1888:* Ran trials. *1901:* Transferred to The Hain Steamship Co. Ltd. *30.8.1905:* Sold for £9,000 to G. & D. Domestinis, Greece and renamed IOANNIS DOMESTINIS. *1907:* Sold to Bank of Athens (K. Hadjipateras, manager), Greece and renamed LEANDROS. *1913:* Sold to C. Hadjipateras and N. & D. Pateras, Greece. *25.8.1916:* Torpedoed and sunk by the German submarine U.38 100 miles E. of Barcelona,in a position 41.52 N, 04.07 E whilst on a voyage from Cardiff to Genoa.

15.   TREWAVAS (1888 — 1892)
O.N. 91346. 1682g, 1054n. 259.0 × 36.1 × 17.9 feet.
T.3-cyl. by the Shipbuilder.
23.7.1888: Launched by J. Readhead and Co., South Shields (Yard No. 239), for Edward Hain and Son. *27.8.1888:* Ran trials. *16.1.1892:* Sailed from Cardiff for Kingston, Jamaica with a cargo of coal and disappeared.

TREWELLARD   *E. N. Taylor*

16.   TREWELLARD (I) (1889 — 1913)
O.N. 91347. 2269g, 1452n. 290.0 × 39.0 × 18.8 feet.
T.3-cyl. by the Shipbuilder.
4.3.1889: Completed by J. Readhead and Sons, South Shields (Yard No. 246), for Edward Hain and Son. *1901:* Transferred to The Hain Steamship Co. Ltd. *29.7.1913:* Sold for £11,000 to D. B. Corpi, Italy and renamed ANTONIO DI PADOVA. *8.12.1913:* Sailed from Zoungouldak, Turkey for Genoa, via Heraclea, with a cargo of wheat and disappeared.

TREVORIAN   E. N. Taylor

17.   TREVORIAN (I) (1889 — 1910)
O.N. 91348. 2270g, 1443n. 290.0 × 39.0 × 18.8 feet.
T.3-cyl. by the Shipbuilder.
30.3.1889: Launched by J. Readhead and Sons, South Shields (Yard No. 247), for Edward Hain
and Son. *29.4.1889:* Ran trials. *1901:* Transferred to The Hain Steamship Co. Ltd. *25.1.1910:*
Foundered in the Bay of Biscay whilst on a voyage from Barry to Taranto with a cargo of coal.

TREGLISSON   E. N. Taylor

32

18. TREGLISSON (I) (1889 — 1911)
O.N. 91349. 2273g, 1461n. 290.2 × 39.1 × 18.8 feet.
T.3-cyl. by the Shipbuilder.
31.8.1889: Launched by J. Readhead and Sons, South Shields (Yard No. 252), for Edward Hain
and Son. *10.1889:* Completed. *1901:* Transferred to The Hain Steamship Co. Ltd. *28.10.1911:*
Sold for £6,000 to Compagnie des Chargeurs Français (Plisson et Cie., managers), France and
renamed HENDAYE. *1926:* Sold to Benvenuto & Mortola, Italy and renamed AQUILA. *1926:*
Renamed REGULUS. *1928:* Sold to shipbreakers.

TREVALGAN   *E. N. Taylor*

19. TREVALGAN (I) (1890 — 1911)
O.N. 98241. 2420g, 1567n. 290.5 × 40.0 × 19.8 feet.
T.3-cyl. by the Shipbuilder.
18.2.1890: Launched by J. Readhead and Sons, South Shields (Yard No. 257), for Edward Hain
and Son. *15.3.1890:* Ran trials. *1901:* Transferred to The Hain Steamship Co. Ltd. *10.5.1911:*
Sold for £7,000 to Compania del Vapor Charito (Uribarri & Echevarria, managers), Spain and
renamed CHARITO. *1915:* Sold to Jose de Uribarri, Spain. *1916:* Sold to Altos Hornos de Vizcaya
S.A. Spain and renamed FAUSTINO R. SAN PEDRO. *28.7.1936:* Requisitioned by Republican
forces for service during the Spanish Civil War. *11.6.1937:* In collision with the steamship MARIA
AMALIA 744/18 off Santander whilst on a voyage from Gijon to Bilbao with coal. She was
beached near Conejera Inlet at the entrance to Suances in a position 43.26 N, 04.02 W and
subsequently sank.

20. TRESILLIAN (I) (1890 — 1896)
O.N. 98242. 2429g, 1570n. 290.5 × 40.0 × 19.8 feet.
T.3-cyl. by the Shipbuilder.
19.3.1890: Launched by J. Readhead and Sons, South Shields (Yard No. 258), for Edward Hain
and Son. *4.1890:* Completed. *22.1.1896:* Wrecked at Hisipezza near Otranto, Italy whilst on a
voyage from Cardiff to Brindisi with a cargo of coal. The salvage steamer BERGER WILHELM was
despatched from Piraeus to assist, but by *27.2.1896* the funnel and bridge were reported washed
overboard and the hatch comings and decks stove in. Subsequently abandoned as a total loss.

TREVAYLOR

21. TREVAYLOR (I) (1890 — 1911)
O.N. 98243. 2426g, 1572n. 290.4 × 40.0 × 19.8 feet.
T.3-cyl. by the Shipbuilder.
20.5.1890: Launched by J. Readhead and Sons, South Shields (Yard No. 260), for Edward Hain and Son. *15.7.1890:* Ran trials. *1901:* Transferred to The Hain Steamship Co. Ltd. *23.5.1911:* Sold for £6,250 to Cosmettos & Filicos, Greece and renamed SIFNOS. *1915:* Sold to D/S A/S Fjoesanger (Frimann & Pedersen, managers), Norway and renamed HALLINGDAL. *1916:* Sold to A/S D/S Hamlet (H. Thomsen, manager), Denmark and renamed AMLETH. *1917:* Sold to A/S D/S Orion (C. P. Jensen, manager), Denmark. *1920:* Renamed POLARIS. *1928:* Sold to Rederi Aktieb. Iris (C. Abrahamsen, manager), Sweden. *1956:* Sold to C. Persson & Son, Sweden, and *30.5.1956* arrived at Ystad to be broken up.

22. TREGURNO (I) (1891 — 1911)
O.N. 98244. 2432g, 1564n. 290.0 × 40.0 × 19.9 feet.
T.3-cyl. by the Shipbuilder.
18.8.1891: Launched by J. Readhead and Sons, South Shields (Yard No. 274), for Edward Hain and Son. *17.9.1891:* Ran trials. *1901:* Transferred to The Hain Steamship Co. Ltd. *10.3.1911:* Sold for £8,000 to Pandeli Bros., Greece and renamed PANDELIS. *1918:* Taken over by The Shipping Controller (Galbraith, Pembroke and Co., managers). *1920:* Returned to owners. *1934:* Sold to Mme. Alexandra Pappadopoulou, Greece and renamed HELLAS. *1934:* Sold to Italian shipbreakers.

TREGURNO   *E. N. Taylor*

34

TREVANION

23. TREVANION (I) (1891 — 1911)
O.N. 98245. 2437g, 1566n. 290.0 × 40.1 × 19.9 feet.
T.3-cyl. by the Shipbuilder.
17.10.1891: Launched by J. Readhead and Sons, South Shields (Yard No. 276), for Edward Hain
and Son. *11.1891:* Completed. *1901:* Transferred to The Hain Steamship Co. Ltd. *27.9.1911:*
Sold for £7,700 to N. M. Emiris, Greece and renamed MICHAIL. *1912:* Sold to J. Trofimoff, Greece.
1916: Registered under A. M. Emiris & J. Trofimoff, Greece. *25.10.1916:* Sailed from Cardiff for
the Azores and after passing the Lizard on *1.11.1916,* disappeared.

24. TREWIDDEN (II) (1891 — 1915)
O.N. 98246. 2613g, 1683n. 298.5 × 40.1 × 20.1 feet.
T.3-cyl. by the Shipbuilder.
30.12.1891: Launched by J. Readhead and Sons, South Shields (Yard No. 278), for Edward Hain
and Son. *2.1892:* Completed. *1901:* Transferred to The Hain Steamship Co. Ltd. *4.9.1915:* Sold
for £29,000 to Gart S.S. Co. Ltd. (Whimster and Co., managers), Glasgow and renamed
GARTLAND. *3.1.1918:* Torpedoed and sunk by the German submarine UB.30, 5 miles E.S.E. from
Owers Light.

TREWIDDEN

TREGENNA

25. TREGENNA (II) (1892 — 1915)
O.N. 98248. 2623g, 1691n. 298.4 × 40.1 × 20.1 feet.
T.3-cyl. by the Shipbuilder.
11.2.1892: Launched by J. Readhead and Sons, South Shields (Yard No. 279), for Edward Hain and Son. *21.4.1892:* Ran trials. *1901:* Transferred to The Hain Steamship Co. Ltd. *15.10.1915:* Sold for £31,000 to Stathe S.S. Co. Ltd. (John Sidney Rees, manager), Cardiff and renamed STATHE. *26.9.1916:* Captured by the German submarine U.35 and sunk by gunfire 50 miles E. by S. from Barcelona. She was on a voyage from Penarth to Leghorn with a cargo of coal.

TREFUSIS

TREFUSIS aground at North Gare, Seaton Carew, in 1902   *K. Ingram Collection*

26.   TREFUSIS (I) (1893 — 1917)
O.N. 98249. 2642g, 1708n. 299.0 × 40.1 × 20.6 feet.
T.3-cyl. by the Shipbuilder.
13.3.1893: Launched by J. Readhead and Sons, South Shields (Yard No. 288), for Edward Hain and Son. *4.1893:* Completed. *1901:* Transferred to The Hain Steamship Co. Ltd. *7.4.1917:* Captured by the German submarine U.65, 30 miles S.E. of Cape Pula, Sardinia, and sunk by explosive charges in position 56.30 N, 32.14 W. She was on a voyage from Cardiff to Alexandria with a cargo of coal.

TREVELYAN   *T. Rayner*

27.   TREVELYAN (I) (1894 — 1918)
O.N. 98250. 3066g, 1986n. 321.5 × 41.5 × 21.8 feet.
T.3-cyl. by the Shipbuilder.
21.3.1894: Launched by J. Readhead and Sons, South Shields (Yard No. 295), for Edward Hain and Son. *4.1894:* Completed. *1901:* Transferred to The Hain Steamship Co. Ltd. *19.12.1917:* Torpedoed and damaged by a German submarine 20 miles N. of Cap Barfleur, France whilst on a voyage from Rouen to Barry. Beached and declared a total loss. *5.4.1918:* Sold for £80,000 to Sicilia Soc. di Nav., Italy, salved and repaired at Cherbourg. *1919:* Renamed ESPERIA. *1920:* Sold to Soc. Anon. di Nav. Orientale, Italy. *1924:* Sold to Italian shipbreakers and broken up at Genoa.

TREVETHOE
E. N. Taylor

28. TREVETHOE (I) (1895 — 1911)
O.N. 104671. 2097g, 1344n. 284.3 × 39.0 × 16.8 feet.
T.3-cyl. by the Shipbuilder.
28.3.1895: Launched by J. Readhead and Sons, South Shields (Yard No. 305), for Edward Hain and Son. *6.5.1895:* Ran trials. *1901:* Transferred to The Hain Steamship Co. Ltd. *27.3.1911:* Sold for £9,300 to Akties. D/S. Erviken (J. Christensen, manager), Norway and renamed ERVIKEN. *1912:* Management transferred to Wallem and Co. *1915:* Management transferred to H. J. Wallem. *25.10.1917:* Torpedoed and sunk by the German submarine U.64 off Cabo de Gata, Spain, whilst on a voyage from San Reggio to Seville.

TREVARRACK
E. N. Taylor

38

29.   TREVARRACK (I) (1895 — 1914)
O.N. 104672. 2098g, 1344n. 284.3 × 39.0 × 16.8 feet.
T.3-cyl. by the Shipbuilder.
30.4.1895: Launched by J. Readhead and Sons, South Shields (Yard No. 306), for Edward Hain and Son. *28.5.1895:* Ran trialc. *1901:* Transferred to The Hain Steamship Co. Ltd. *27.6.1914:* Sold for £11,000 to Rederiaktieb. Rekord (A. L. Nilsson, manager), Sweden and renamed IRIS. *25.12.1917:* Wrecked off the Longsands, Essex whilst on a voyage from Gothenburg to Rouen with general cargo.

TREVOSE   *E. N. Taylor*

30.   TREVOSE (II) (1896 — 1917)
O.N. 104673. 3112g, 1995n. 323.5 × 47.1 × 22.6 feet.
T.3-cyl. by the Shipbuilder.
18.3.1896: Launched by J. Readhead and Sons, South Shields (Yard No. 314), for Trevose Steamship Co. Ltd. (Edward Hain and Son, managers). *4.1896:* Completed. *1901:* Transferred to The Hain Steamship Co. Ltd. *18.3.1917:* Torpedoed and sunk by the German submarine U.81, 230 miles W. by N.$\frac{1}{4}$N. from Ushant whilst outward bound from the River Tyne with a cargo of coal.

31.   TREVILLEY (II) (1897 — 1911)
O.N. 104674. 3112g, 1983n. 323.0 × 47.1 × 22.6 feet.
T.3-cyl. by the Shipbuilder.
1.3.1897: Launched by J. Readhead and Sons, South Shields (Yard No. 322), for Trevilley Steamship Co. Ltd. (Edward Hain and Son, managers). *30.3.1897:* Ran trials. *1901:* Transferred to The Hain Steamship Co. Ltd. *20.1.1911:* Seriously damaged in collision with the German steamship SANTA LUCIA 4,238/07 off Krankeloon in the River Scheldt. A large hole was torn in her port side and she was beached to avoid sinking. *11.2.1911:* Refloated and towed to Siberia Dock, Antwerp, for drydocking. She had been on a voyage from Bourgas to Antwerp with grain. Repairs were considered uneconomical and sold *31.3.1911* for 127,500 Belgian Francs to Antwerp Engineering Co. Ltd., Belgium. *7.1911:* Sold to Anglo-Ionian S.S. Co. Ltd. (A. A. Embiricos & Co., managers), Greece and renamed SALAMINIA. *1917:* Sold to Embiricos & Drosopulos Maritime Co. Ltd., Greece. *1917:* Sold to Hellenic Shipowning Co. Ltd., Greece. *29.3.1918:* Torpedoed and sunk off Anglesey in a position 53.27 N, 05.32 W.

TRELYON   W.S.P.L.

32. TRELYON (II) (1897 — 1917)
O.N. 104675. 3099g, 1990n. 323.0 × 47.0 × 22.5 feet.
T.3-cyl. by the Shipbuilder.
25.11.1897: Launched by J. Readhead and Sons, South Shields (Yard No. 329), for Trelyon
Steamship Co. Ltd., (Edward Hain and Son, managers). *26.1.1898:* Ran trials. *1901:* Transferred
to The Hain Steamship Co. Ltd. *21.7.1917:* Mined 3 miles N. of Scarborough whilst on a voyage
from Archangel, Russia, to the U.K. with a cargo of timber. Beached at White Nab, Scarborough
and became a total loss.

TREKIEVE   E. N. Taylor

33. TREKIEVE (II) (1898 — 1917)
O.N. 104676. 3087g, 1983n. 323.0 × 47.1 × 22.6 feet.
T.3-cyl. by the Shipbuilder.
4.6.1898: Launched by J. Readhead and Sons, South Shields (Yard No. 332), for Trekieve
Steamship Co. Ltd., (Edward Hain and Son, managers). *23.7.1898:* Ran trials. *1901:* Transferred
to The Hain Steamship Co. Ltd. *18.4.1917:* Torpedoed and sunk by the German submarine U.35,
100 miles W. of Gibraltar whilst on a voyage from Cardiff to Gibraltar with Government cargo.

40

TRESILLIAN   *K. Ingram Collection*

34.   TRESILLIAN (II) (1899 — 1924)
O.N. 104677. 3585g, 2309n. 341.0 × 46.7 × 26.0 feet.
T.3-cyl. by the Shipbuilder.
27.7.1899: Launched by J. Readhead and Sons, South Shields (Yard No. 341), for Tresillian Steamship Co. Ltd., (Edward Hain and Son, managers). *8.1899:* Completed. *1901:* Transferred to The Hai— Steamship Co. Ltd. *9.4.1924:* Sold to Monument Steam Navigation Co. Ltd., London and renamed YORKHILL. *1926:* Sold to Naigai Kisen K.K., Japan and renamed TAISEI MARU. *5.6.1944:* Sunk in a collision off Komoi Cape, Hokkaido, Japan.

TREVESSA

35.   TREVESSA (I) (1899 — 1920)
O.N. 104678. 3566g, 2296n. 341.0 × 46.7 × 26.0 feet.
T.3-cyl. by the Shipbuilder.
6.9.1899: Launched by J. Readhead and Sons, South Shields (Yard No. 342), for Trevessa Steamship Co. Ltd., (Edward Hain and Son, managers). *10.1899:* Completed. *1901:* Transferred to The Hain Steamship Co. Ltd. *28.8.1920:* Sold for £90,000 to Sociedad Nacional de Buques y Maderas, Chile and renamed MIRAMAR. *9.6.1926:* Wrecked at Valparaiso during a severe gale.

41

TREVIDER   *Raul Maya Collection*

36. TREVIDER (II) (1902 — 1911)
O.N. 115641. 3082g, 1990n. 323.0 × 47.0 × 23.6 feet.
T. 3-cyl. by the Shipbuilder.
6.8.1902: Launched by J. Readhead and Sons, South Shields (Yard No. 363), for The Hain
Steamship Co. Ltd. *8.9.1902:* Ran trials. *28.4.1911:* Wrecked off Cabo Villano, Spain, whilst on
a voyage from Newport, Mon. to Palermo with a cargo of coal.

37. TRELOSKE (II) (1902 — 1917)
O.N. 115642. 3071g, 1976n. 323.0 × 47.0 × 23.7 feet.
T. 3-cyl. by the Shipbuilder.
6.9.1902: Launched by J. Readhead and Sons, South Shields (Yard No. 364), for The Hain
Steamship Co. Ltd. *9.10.1902:* Ran trials. *29.8.1917:* Torpedoed and sunk by the German
submarine U.93, 145 miles N. by W.¾W. from Cape Finisterre whilst on a voyage from Barry to
Spezia with a cargo of coal.

TREVEAN   *E. N. Taylor*

38. TREVEAN (II) (1902 — 1917)
O.N. 115643. 3081g, 1989n. 323.0 × 47.1 × 23.7 feet.
T. 3-cyl. by the Shipbuilder.
15.10.1902: Launched by J. Readhead and Sons, South Shields (Yard No. 365), for The Hain
Steamship Co. Ltd. *17.11.1902:* Ran trials. *22.1.1917:* Captured by the German submarine U.57
and sunk by bombs 240 miles S.W. by W. from Fastnet. She was on a voyage from Benisaf, Algeria,
to the River Tyne with a cargo of iron ore.

TREGANTLE

39. TREGANTLE (I) (1902 — 1916)
O.N. 115644. 3091g, 1991n. 323.0 × 47.1 × 23.7 feet.
T. 3-cyl. by the Shipbuilder.
17.11.1902: Launched by J. Readhead and Sons, South Shields (Yard No. 366), for The Hain Steamship Co. Ltd. *17.1.1903:* Ran trials. *22.4.1916:* Torpedoed and sunk by the German submarine UB.16, 1¼ miles E.S.E. from Corton Light Vessel whilst on a voyage from Galveston and Norfolk, Virginia, to Hull with a cargo of wheat.

40. TREWYN (I) (1903 — 1916)
O.N. 115645. 3084g, 1989n. 323.0 × 47.1 × 23.7 feet.
T. 3-cyl. by the Shipbuilder.
15.1.1903: Launched by J. Readhead and Sons, South Shields (Yard No. 367), for The Hain Steamship Co. Ltd. *9.3.1903:* Ran trials. *25.3.1916:* Passed Gibraltar whilst on a voyage from Algiers to Middlesbrough with a cargo of iron ore and subsequently disappeared. On 1.4.1916 a lifebuoy and other wreckage was sighted, but no survivors.

TREWYN

41. TREGOTHNAN (I) (1903 — 1923)
O.N. 115646. 3075g, 1983n. 323.0 × 47.1 × 23.7 feet.
T. 3-cyl. by the Shipbuilder.
12.3.1903: Launched by J. Readhead and Sons, South Shields (Yard No. 368), for The Hain Steamship Co. Ltd. *20.4.1903:* Ran trials. *1.8.1923:* Sold to Strick Line (1923) Ltd. (F. C. Strick and Co. Ltd., managers), London. *1926:* Transferred to The Dwina Ltd. (same managers), London. *1928:* Sold to S. A. M. Killingbeck (M. Xydia, manager), Egypt. *1932:* Sold to Samy Khouri (Costi Xydia & Son, managers), Egypt. *1935:* Sold to Basile Sapovalos, Greece. *1939:* Sold to Palestine Transport and Shipping Co. Ltd. (N. W. Purvis, manager), Palestine, and renamed HAIFA TRADER. *1941:* Sold to Irish Shipping Ltd., Eire, and renamed IRISH LARCH. *1949:* Sold to Mehmet Hilmi Daregenli Sirketi, Turkey, and renamed SABAH. *1950:* Registered under Hilmi Daregenli, Turkey.

TREGOTHNAN   *T. Rayner*

1952: Registered under Fuad Muradoglu ve Hilmi Daregenli Vapurculuk Sirketi, Turkey. *1958:* Sold to Sadikzade Nazim Ogullari Vapurculuk Komandit Sirketi, Turkey, and renamed KERVAN. *1961:* Sold to Fratelli Cosulich, Italy and 27.7.1961 arrived at Trieste to be broken up.

TREGARTHEN   *E. N. Taylor*

42.   TREGARTHEN (I) (1904 — 1911)
O.N. 115647. 2171g, 1376n. 289.0 × 43.0 × 20.1 feet.
T. 3-cyl. by the Shipbuilder.
17.2.1904: Launched by J. Readhead and Sons, South Shields (Yard No. 375), for The Hain Steamship Co. Ltd. *21.3.1904:* Ran trials. *15.8.1911:* Sold for £16,350 to Delmas Frères, France, and renamed FRANK DELMAS. *1920:* Registered under Compagnie Delmas Frères & Vieljeux, France. *1933:* Sold to J. D. Chandris, Greece, and renamed MARI CHANDRIS. *1936:* Sold to Rederi A/B Snabb (Algot Johansson, manager), Finland, and renamed SNABB. *3.6.1940:* Torpedoed and sunk by the German submarine U.37, 300 miles off Cape Finisterre. She was on a voyage from Greenock to Dakar. One crew member was killed and the remainder were landed at Queenstown.

44

TREMATON

E. N. Taylor

43. TREMATON (I) (1904 — 1911)
O.N. 115648. 2171g, 1374n. 289.2 × 43.0 × 20.2 feet.
T. 3-cyl. by the Shipbuilder.
19.3.1904: Launched by J. Readhead and Sons, South Shields (Yard No. 376), for The Hain
Steamship Co. Ltd. *28.4.1904:* Ran trials. *27.6.1911:* Sold for £16,200 to Compania Naviera
Vascongada (F. de Abasolo, manager), Spain and renamed ARTAGAN. *29.2.1912:* Wrecked off
Carboeiros, Cape Verde Islands, whilst on a voyage from Cardiff to Barcelona with a cargo of coal.

44. TREMEADOW (I) (1905 — 1917)
O.N. 115649. 3653g, 2358n. 347.2 × 49.1 × 25.1 feet.
T. 3-cyl. by the Shipbuilder.
2.2.1905: Launched by J. Readhead and Sons, South Shields (Yard No. 383), for The Hain
Steamship Co. Ltd. *6.3.1905:* Ran trials. *19.1.1917:* Captured by the German submarine UC.21
and sunk by gunfire 35 miles N.E.¾N. from Ushant, France. She was on a voyage from Buenos
Aires to Hull with a cargo of maize.

TREMORVAH on trials, April 1905

K. Ingram Collection

45. TREMORVAH (I) (1905 — 1917)
O.N. 115650. 3654g, 2345n. 347.3 × 49.1 × 25.1 feet.
T. 3-cyl. by the Shipbuilder.
7.3.1905: Launched by J. Readhead and Sons, South Shields (Yard No. 384), for The Hain
Steamship Co. Ltd. *4.1905:* Completed. *11.4.1917:* Captured by the German submarine U.65
and sunk by gunfire 70 miles N.N.W. from Cape Bougaroni, Algeria, whilst on a voyage from Malta
to Gibraltar in ballast.

46. TRENEGLOS (III) (1906 — 1915)
O.N. 122651. 3886g, 2510n. 346.4 × 49.5 × 26.5 feet.
T. 3-cyl. by the Shipbuilder.
9.2.1906: Launched by J. Readhead and Sons, South Shields (Yard No. 391), for The Hain Steamship Co. Ltd. *3.1906:* Completed. *14.11.1915:* Torpedoed and sunk by the German submarine U.34, 70 miles W.S.W. from Gavdo Island, Crete, whilst homeward bound from Mauritius with a cargo of sugar.

TREMAYNE

47. TREMAYNE (II) (1906 — 1926)
O.N. 122652. 3881g, 2507n. 346.3 × 49.6 × 26.5 feet.
T. 3-cyl. by the Shipbuilder.
22.3.1906: Launched by J. Readhead and Sons, South Shields (Yard No. 392), for The Hain Steamship Co. Ltd. *7.5.1906:* Ran trials. *1926:* Sold for £23,500 to Kingdom Steamships Ltd. (Jackson Brothers, managers), London, and renamed COLLINGDALE. *13.4.1927:* Wrecked near Melilla, Spanish North Africa, whilst on a voyage from Melilla to Rotterdam with a cargo of iron ore.

TRELAWNY sinking after collision in thick fog 15th July 1926. Believed photographed from GAELIC PRINCE
K. Ingram Collection

48. TRELAWNY (II) (1906 — 1926)
O.N. 122653. 3877g, 2502n. 346.0 × 49.6 × 26.5 feet.
T. 3-cyl. by the Shipbuilder.
15.12.1906: Launched by J. Readhead and Sons, South Shields (Yard No. 398), for The Hain Steamship Co. Ltd. *2.1907:* Completed. *15.7.1926:* Sank in the North Atlantic in position 48.44 N, 17.56 W, following a collision with the British steamship GAELIC PRINCE, 8634/18, whilst on a voyage from Rotterdam to Hampton Roads in ballast.

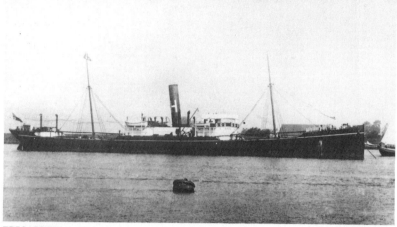

TRECARRELL   *J. Behenna Collection*

49.   TRECARRELL (I) (1907 — 1916)
O.N. 122654. 3875g, 2502n. 346.0 × 49.6 × 26.5 feet.
T. 3-cyl. by the Shipbuilder.
11.2.1907: Launched by J. Readhead and Sons, South Shields (Yard No. 399), for The Hain
Steamship Co. Ltd. *3.1907:* Completed. *24.2.1916:* Wrecked on Black Fish Shoal, Chincoteague
Island, Virginia, whilst on a voyage from Huelva to Philadelphia with a cargo of pyrites.

TREVINCE   *T. Rayner*

50.   TREVINCE (I) (1907 — 1926)
O.N. 122655. 3874g, 2502n. 346.0 × 49.6 × 26.5 feet.
T. 3-cyl. by the Shipbuilder.
19.3.1907: Launched by J. Readhead and Sons, South Shields (Yard No. 400), for The Hain
Steamship Co. Ltd. *25.4.1907:* Ran trials. *1926:* Sold for £20,000 to Cassar Co. Ltd., Malta, and
renamed CASSAR. Resold to J. Pateras, Greece, and renamed IOANNIS PATERAS. *1927:*
Registered under N. J. Pateras and Sons, Greece. *1930:* Renamed SAPPHO. *10.6.1932:* Wrecked
W. of the Burlings on the Portuguese coast whilst on a voyage from Bona, Algeria, to Stettin,
Germany, with a cargo of phosphate.

47

TRELISSICK   *South Tyneside Museum*

51.   TRELISSICK (I) (1909 — 1917)
O.N. 122656. 4168g, 2647n. 363.4 × 51.1 × 26.1 feet.
T.3-cyl. by the Shipbuilder.
6.7.1909: Launched by J. Readhead and Sons Ltd., South Shields (Yard No. 408), for The Hain
Steamship Co. Ltd. *8.1909:* Completed. *15.7.1917:* Torpedoed and sunk by the German
submarine UC.72, 80 miles S.W. by W.¼W. from Ushant, whilst on a voyage from Boston to
Bordeaux with a cargo of oats and steel.

52.   TREVEAL (I) (1909 — 1918)
O.N. 122657. 4160g, 2641n. 363.4 × 51.0 × 26.1 feet.
T.3-cyl. by the Shipbuilder.
30.9.1909: Launched by J. Readhead and Sons Ltd., South Shields (Yard No. 410), for The Hain
Steamship Co. Ltd. *4.11.1909:* Ran trials. *4.2.1918:* Torpedoed and sunk by the German
submarine U.35 off the Skerries, Anglesey whilst on a voyage from Algiers to Barrow with a cargo
of iron ore.

TREVEAL   *F. W. Hawks*

53.   TREVERBYN (I) (1910 — 1917)
O.N. 122658. 4163g, 2642n. 363.2 × 51.0 × 26.1 feet.
T.3-cyl. by the Shipbuilder.
9.2.1910: Launched by J. Readhead and Sons Ltd., South Shields (Yard No. 412), for The Hain
Steamship Co. Ltd. *16.3.1910:* Ran trials. *3.9.1917:* Mined and sunk 2 miles E.S.E. from Ushinish
Light, South Uist, whilst on a voyage from North Russia to Manchester with a cargo of iron ore.

The launch of **TREVERBYN** on 9th February 1910   *K. Ingram Collection*

54.   TREVORIAN (II) (1911 — 1914)
O.N. 122659. 4144g, 2642n. 363.0 × 51.0 × 26.1 feet.
T.3-cyl. by the Shipbuilder.
15.3.1911: Launched by J. Readhead and Sons Ltd., South Shields (Yard No. 418), for The Hain Steamship Co. Ltd. *4.1911:* Completed. *8.1914:* Detained by Russian forces in the Black Sea and subsequently requisitioned as Transport No. 68. *12.2.1917:* Sold for £135,000 to The Lords Commissioners of the Admiralty who 13.2.1917 requested that the Register be closed. *26.12.1918:* Returned to the British Government. *19.5.1919:* Wrecked at Anatolia Lighthouse in the Black Sea when in tow from Novorossisk to Constantinople.

55.   TREGURNO (II) (1911 — 1930)
O.N. 122660. 4145g, 2646n. 363.0 × 51.1 × 26.1 feet.
T.3-cyl. by the Shipbuilder.
1.5.1911: Launched by J. Readhead and Sons Ltd., South Shields (Yard No. 419), for The Hain Steamship Co. Ltd. *1.6.1911:* Ran trials. *1930:* Sold for £25,500 to C. D. Calafatis, Greece and renamed MEROPI. *1932:* Sold to A. Pappas, Greece. *15.2.1942:* Torpedoed and sunk by the German submarine U.566 off Halifax, N.S. in a position 44.14 N, 62.41 W whilst on a voyage from the River Tyne to Halifax. 24 crew and 2 gunners were lost.

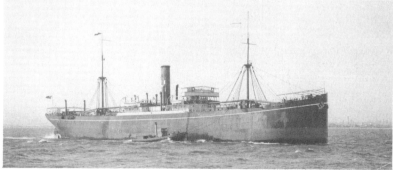

TREVALGAN   *V. Brownlie*

56.   TREVALGAN (II) (1911 — 1929)
O.N. 133211. 4185g, 2675n. 363.0 × 51.1 × 26.1 feet.
T.3-cyl. by the Shipbuilder.
26.7.1911: Launched by J. Readhead and Sons Ltd., South Shields (Yard No. 421), for The Hain

Steamship Co. Ltd. *9.1911:* Completed. *1929:* Sold for £27,750 to N. G. Kyriakides, Greece and renamed GEORGIOS KYRIAKIDES. *1937:* Registered under the Heirs of the late N. G. Kyriakides, Greece. *30.6.1940:* Torpedoed and sunk by the German submarine U.47, S.W. of Cape Clear in a position 50.25 N, 14.33 W whilst on a voyage from Macoris, St. Domingo to Liverpool with a cargo of sugar in bags. The crew of 30 were saved.

TREVANION

57. TREVANION (II) (1912 — 1929)
O.N. 133212. 4267g, 2727n. 369.7 × 51.1 × 26.1 feet.
T.3-cyl. by the Shipbuilder.
2.3.1912: Launched by J. Readhead and Sons Ltd., South Shields (Yard No. 425), for The Hain Steamship Co. Ltd. *11.4.1912:* Ran trials. *1929:* Sold for £24,500 to Proios Brothers, Greece, and renamed MAROULA. *29.11.1934:* Wrecked near Necochea, Argentine Republic whilst on a voyage from Brindisi to Necochea in ballast.

TREGLISSON   *A. Duncan*

58. TREGLISSON (II) (1912 — 1914)(1919 — 1934)
O.N. 133213. 4265g, 2727n. 369.8 × 51.1 × 26.1 feet.
T.3-cyl. by the Shipbuilder.
30.9.1912: Launched by J. Readhead and Sons Ltd., South Shields (Yard No. 429), for The Hain Steamship Co. Ltd. *11.1912:* Completed. *4.8.1914:* Detained at Bremen whilst discharging a cargo of barley and rye from Taganrog, Russia. Served as a prison ship. *20.1.1919:* Returned to owners. *1934:* Sold for £8,350 to Neptun Sea Navigation Co. Ltd. (B. Burger, manager), Hungary and renamed NYUGAT. *1940:* Sold to Soc. Anon. Maritime et Commerciale, Panama and renamed LIRAN. *1941:* Seized by Dutch authorities off Timor. *2.3.1942:* Scuttled at Sourabaya.

50

TREVAYLOR arriving at Waterford   J. Hartery

59. TREVAYLOR (II) (1912 — 1934)
O.N. 133214. 4249g, 2717n. 369.9 × 51.1 × 26.1 feet.
T.3-cyl. by the Shipbuilder.
7.11.1912: Launched by J. Readhead and Sons Ltd., South Shields (Yard No. 430), for The Hain
Steamship Co. Ltd. *12.1912:* Completed. *1934:* Sold for £8,875 to Lensen Transport Ltd.
(Cornelis A. Lensen, manager), London and renamed FREDERIKA LENSEN. *1940:* Sold to Austin
Friars Steam Shipping Co. Ltd. (Galbraith, Pembroke and Co., managers), London. *20.7.1942:*
Torpedoed by the German submarine U.132 in a position 49.22 N, 65.12 W whilst on a voyage
from Montreal to Sydney N.S. in ballast. Subsequently beached in Grand Valee Bay where she
broke her back and was declared a constructive total loss. Four crew were lost.

TREVETHOE   A. Duncan

60. TREVETHOE (II) (1913 — 1932)
O.N. 133215. 4248g, 2716n. 369.9 × 51.1 × 26.1 feet.
T.3-cyl. by the Shipbuilder.
8.1.1913: Launched by J. Readhead and Sons Ltd., South Shields (Yard No. 431), for The Hain
Steamship Co. Ltd. *2.1913:* Completed. *1932:* Sold for £8,250 to N. V. Scheepvaart Maats.
Houtvervoer, Panama, and renamed ANTJE CATHARINA. *1933:* Sold to Atlantic Tank-Rhederei
G.m.b.H. (J. T. Essberger, G.m.b.H., managers), Germany and renamed KARIN. *1936:* Sold to
Kauffahrtei A.G., later Kauffahrtei Seereederei Adolf Wiards & Co., Germany, and renamed
EMSHORN. *21.12.1941:* Torpedoed and sunk by the Russian submarine M.174 at Petsamo,
Russia.

TREVILLEY, 13th January 1932   *John G. Callis*

61. TREVILLEY (III) (1913 — 1932)
O.N. 133216. 4259g, 2724n. 369.9 × 51.1 × 26.1 feet.
T.3-cyl. by the Shipbuilder.
22.2.1913: Launched by J. Readhead and Sons Ltd., South Shields (Yard No. 432), for The Hain
Steamship Co. Ltd. *4.1913:* Completed. *1932:* Sold for £7,350 to Osterreichischer Lloyd
Schiffahrts A.G., Austria, and renamed WIEN. *1933:* Sold to Slobodna Plovidba Topić D.D. (Ant.
Topić, manager), Yugoslavia, and renamed SERAFIN TOPIC. *1941:* Interned at Oran by the French
authorities and *11.1942* taken over by the Italian Government and renamed COSALA. *10.2.1943:*
Torpedoed and sunk by H.M.S. UNA about 7 miles off Punta Staletti, whilst on a voyage from
Messina to Taranto.

62. TREVIDER (III) (1913 — 1914)(1919 — 1933)
O.N. 133217. 4260g, 2723n. 369.9 × 51.1 × 26.1 feet.
T.3-cyl. by the Shipbuilder.
9.4.1913: Launched by J. Readhead and Sons Ltd., South Shields (Yard No. 433), for The Hain
Steamship Co. Ltd. *5.1913:* Completed. *4.8.1914:* Detained at Brake, Germany, whilst
discharging a cargo of barley from Taganrog and Novorossisk, Russia. *18.12.1918:* Returned to
owners. *1933:* Sold for £8,350 to "Ilirija" Dionicko Drustvo za Brodarstvo (Ant. Topić, manager),
Yugoslavia and renamed ROSINA TOPIC. *1934:* Owners restyled "Ilirija" Navigation Co. Ltd.,
(same managers). *1.3.1941:* Time chartered to the Ministry of Shipping (later Ministry of War
Transport), registered at Belfast and renamed PICOTEE. H. Hogarth and Sons appointed managers.
7.8.1947: Returned to Brodarsko Akcionarsko Drustvo "Oceania", Yugoslavia, and renamed
ROSINA TOPIC. *1946:* Renamed LIKA. *1947:* Taken over by State Enterprise Jugoslovenska
Slobodna Plovidba, Yugoslavia. *1953:* Sold to Brodospas, Yugoslavia, and broken up at Split.

TREVIDER

TREGARTHEN

63. TREGARTHEN (II) (1913 — 1933)
O.N. 133218. 4263g, 2726n. 369.8 × 51.1 × 26.1 feet.
T.3-cyl. by the Shipbuilder.
22.5.1913: Launched by J. Readhead and Sons Ltd., South Shields (Yard No. 434), for The Hain
Steamship Co. Ltd. *6.1913:* Completed. *1933:* Sold for £6,050 to Neptun Sea Navigation Co.
Ltd., (B. Burger, manager), Hungary and renamed KELET. *19.8.1940:* Torpedoed and sunk by the
German submarine UA in an approximate position 50 N, 22 W, whilst on a voyage from Port Talbot
to Tampa in ballast. Her crew of 33 was rescued.

64. TREWELLARD (II) (1914 — 1933)
O.N. 133219. 4202g, 2667n. 370.2 × 51.6 × 25.0 feet.
T.3-cyl. by the Shipbuilder.
27.5.1914: Launched by J. Readhead and Sons Ltd., South Shields (Yard No. 442), for The Hain
Steamship Co. Ltd. *13.7.1914:* Ran trials. *1933:* Sold for £7,500 to J. D. McLaren and Co.
(Shipping) Ltd., A. A. Callergis & N. G. Revelis, Greece and renamed SYLVA. *1937:* Sold for
£30,000 to Ch. N. Pateras & Co. Greece and renamed VICTORIA. *30.10.1940:* Bombed by
German aircraft N.W. of Rockall in position 54.47 N, 13.32 W, whilst on a voyage from Durban
to Belfast with 7500 tons of sugar. She sank later the same day in position 54.48 N, 13.28 W.
Her crew of 29 was rescued.

TREWELLARD leaving Hamburg, 6th January 1930, having discharged a
cargo of bulk grain from Odessa   *K. Ingram Collection*

65. TREMATON (II) (1914 — 1916)
O.N. 133220. 4198g, 2665n. 370.2 × 51.6 × 25.0 feet.
T.3-cyl. by the Shipbuilder.
23.7.1914: Launched by J. Readhead and Sons Ltd., South Shields (Yard No. 443), for The Hain
Steamship Co. Ltd. *9.1914:* Completed. *20.1.1916:* Captured by the German submarine U.35
and sunk by gunfire 180 miles E. by S. from Malta whilst on a voyage from Karachi to London
with a cargo of grain.

TREVARRACK   *K. Ingram Collection*

66. TREVARRACK (II) (1914 — 1916)
O.N. 137861. 4199g, 2679n. 370.0 × 51.6 × 25.0 feet.
T. 3-cyl. by the Shipbuilder.
21.10.1914: Launched by J. Readhead and Sons Ltd., South Shields (Yard No. 445), for The Hain
Steamship Co. Ltd. *12.1914:* Completed. *16.11.1916:* Captured by the German submarine UC.18
and sunk by gunfire 25 miles W.$\frac{1}{2}$N. from Les Hanois, Guernsey, whilst on a voyage from Buenos
Aires to Hull with a cargo of maize.

67. TRECARNE (I) (1914 — 1933)
O.N. 137862. 4196g, 2679n. 370.3 × 51.6 × 25.0 feet.
T. 3-cyl. by the Shipbuilder.
17.12.1914: Launched by J. Readhead and Sons Ltd., South Shields (Yard No. 446), for The Hain
Steamship Co. Ltd. *2.1915:* Completed. *1933:* Sold for £7,750 to S. Castanos & Sons, Greece,
and renamed STYLIANOS CASTANOS. *9.9.1934:* Stranded West of Oran whilst on a voyage from
Pitea, Sweden to Alexandria, Egypt with a cargo of timber. Subsequently refloated and *8.12.1934*
arrived at Algiers but found to be severely damaged and sold to Italian shipbreakers.

TRECARNE entering Bremen, August 1924   *K. Ingram Collection*

54

68. TREHAWKE (1915 — 1925)
O.N. 137863. 4198g, 2680n. 370.0 × 51.6 × 25.0 feet.
T. 3-cyl. by the Shipbuilder.
17.2.1915: Launched by J. Readhead and Sons Ltd., South Shields (Yard No. 447), for The Hain
Steamship Co. Ltd. *4.1915:* Completed. *17.4.1925:* Wrecked in the Straits of Magellan whilst
on a voyage from Santos to Coronel in ballast.

TREHAWKE   *T. Rayner*

69. TREWIDDEN (III) (1917 — 1937)
O.N. 137867. 4381g, 2776n. 400.0 × 52.1 × 25.2 feet.
T. 3-cyl. by the Shipbuilder.
1917: Launched by J. Readhead and Sons Ltd., South Shields (Yard No. 454), for The Hain
Steamship Co. Ltd. *9.1917:* Completed. *1937:* Sold for £30, 00 to Prekomorska Plovidba D.D.,
Yugoslavia, and renamed KUPA. *15.5.1942:* Torpedoed and sunk by the German submarine U.156
E. of St. Lucia in a position 14.50 N, 52.20 W whilst on a voyage from New York to Table Bay
and Alexandria with a cargo of military trucks, aeroplane parts and oil in drums. Two of her crew
of 41 were lost.

TREWIDDEN in the Manchester Ship Canal

70. TREGENNA (III) (1917)
O.N. 137868. 5772g, 3706n. 400.1 × 52.1 × 33.2 feet.
T. 3-cyl. by the Shipbuilder.
1917: Launched by J. Readhead and Sons Ltd., South Shields (Yard No. 455), for The Hain Steamship Co. Ltd. *12.1917:* Completed. *26.12.1917:* Torpedoed and sunk by the German submarine UB.57, 9 miles South from Dodman Point whilst on her maiden voyage from the River Tyne to Gibraltar with a cargo of coal.

71. TRENEGLOS (IV) (1917 — 1935)
O.N. 137869. 5768g, 3702n. 400.0 × 52.1 × 33.2 feet.
T. 3-cyl. by the Shipbuilder.
14.11.1917: Launched by J. Readhead and Sons Ltd., South Shields (Yard No. 456), for The Hain Steamship Co. Ltd. *3.1918:* Completed. *1935:* Sold for £17,625 to M. J. Lyras and Co., Greece, and renamed GALAXIAS. *1938:* Sold to Galaxias S.S. Co. Ltd., Greece. *23.5.1940:* Bombed and sunk by German aircraft at Dieppe. *14.9.1949:* Reported raised in sections and by *7.1.1950* the final 150 tons had been raised and broken up.

TRENEGLOS *K. Ingram Collection*

72. TREVOSE (III) (1918 — 1935)
O.N. 137870. 5768g, 3702n. 400.2 × 52.1 × 33.2 feet.
T. 3-cyl. by the Shipbuilder.
28.1.1918: Launched by J. Readhead and Sons Ltd., South Shields (Yard No. 457), for The Hain Steamship Co. Ltd. *5.1918:* Completed. *1935:* Sold for £19,500 to Slobodna Plovidba Topić D.D. (Ant. Topić, manager), Yugoslavia, and renamed OLGA TOPIC. *1946:* Sold to Dubrovacka Plovidba A.D., Yugoslavia, and renamed KOSMAJ. *1947:* Taken over by State Enterprise Jugoslovenska Slobodna Plovidba, Yugoslavia. *25.2.1950:* Abandoned on fire S.E. of St. Paul Rocks in a position 03.40 S, 30.15 W, whilst on a voyage from Rosario to Rotterdam with a cargo of linseed. The fire was extinguished *10.3.1950* but on *21.3.1950* broke out again, and all upperworks were reported destroyed. Towed into Fortaleza, Brazil, and on *13.4.1950* was settled as a constructive total loss. The vessel was then abandoned.

TREVOSE *J. Clarkson*

73. TREGANTLE (II) (1918 — 1939)
O.N. 142563. 5742g, 4279n. 400.2 × 52.1 × 33.2 feet.
T. 3-cyl. by the Shipbuilder.
1918: Launched by J. Readhead and Sons Ltd., South Shields (Yard No. 458), for The Hain Steamship Co. Ltd. *10.1918:* Completed. *1939:* Sold for £26,750 to J. G. P. Livanos (J. Livanos and Sons Ltd., managers), Greece, and renamed ANNITSA. *15.1.1943:* Torpedoed and sunk by the German submarine U.617 in a position 33.02 N, 21.58 E, when on passage from Alexandria to Benghazi and Tobruk with a cargo of 4400 tons of petrol in cases. An earlier attempt to discharge at Benghazi had been abandoned owing to a severe gale. One of her crew of 32 and two gunners were lost.

TREGANTLE   *Welsh Industrial & Maritime Museum*

74. TRELOSKE (III) (1918 — 1939)
O.N. 142564. 5767g, 4304n. 400.2 × 52.1 × 33.2 feet.
T. 3-cyl. by the Shipbuilder.
23.10.1918: Launched by J. Readhead and Sons Ltd., South Shields (Yard No. 459), for The Hain Steamship Co. Ltd. *12.1918:* Completed. *1939:* Sold for £27,250 to C. N. Pateras, Greece, and renamed AGIOI VICTORES. *1948:* Sold to Agioi Victores Shipping Co. Ltd., Greece. *1949:* Sold to Elias N. Pateras, Greece, and renamed PARALOS. *1952:* Sold to British Iron and Steel Corporation, allocated to Clayton and Davie Ltd. and *29.12.1952* arrived at Dunston on Tyne to be broken up.

TRELOSKE   *Welsh Industrial & Maritime Museum*

75. TREVEAN (III) (1919 — 1931)
O.N. 142624. 5225g, 3217n. 400.2 × 52.3 × 28.5 feet.
T. 3-cyl. by North Eastern Marine Engineering Co. Ltd., Newcastle.
27.5.1918: Launched by Northumberland Shipbuilding Co. Ltd., Newcastle (Yard No. 249), as WAR QUAIL for The Shipping Controller (Federal Steam Navigation Co. Ltd., managers). *8.1918:* Completed. *1919:* Purchased by The Hain Steamship Co. Ltd. and renamed TREVEAN. *25.2.1931:* Stranded 8 miles East of Anatolia Lighthouse whilst on a voyage from Nicolaieff to Oran with a cargo of ore. *23.5.1931:* Refloated and condemned as a constructive total loss and settled with the underwriters for £35,000. Subsequently sold to Italian shipbreakers for £1,650 and broken up at Trieste.

TREVEAN   *T. Rayner*

TREMEADOW   *E. N. Taylor*

76. TREMEADOW (II) (1919 — 1938)
O.N. 142565. 5302g, 3231n. 400.4 × 52.2 × 28.4 feet.
T. 3-cyl. by the Shipbuilder.
19.12.1918: Launched by D. and W. Henderson and Co. Ltd., Glasgow (Yard No. 516), as WAR PICOTEE for The Shipping Controller (Federal Steam Navigation Co. Ltd., managers). *1919:* Purchased and *3.1919* completed as TREMEADOW for The Hain Steamship Co. Ltd. *1938:* Sold for £31,400 to Biagio Borriello (Lauro & Montella, managers), Italy, and renamed SAGITTA. *9.11.1941:* Attacked by British warships and sunk by gunfire approximately 120 miles S.E. of Punta Stilo, Italy, in a position 37.08 N, 18.09 E, whilst on a voyage from Naples to Tripoli.

77. TREMORVAH (II) (1919 — 1938)
O.N. 142566. 5270g, 3198n. 400.0 × 52.3 × 28.4 feet.
T. 3-cyl. by the Shipbuilder.
18.3.1919: Launched by D. and W. Henderson and Co. Ltd., Glasgow (Yard No. 518), as WAR
PALM for The Shipping Controller (Quito Shipping Company, managers). Purchased and *4.1919*
completed as TREMORVAH for The Hain Steamship Co. Ltd. *1938:* Sold for £31,250 to "Nivose"
Societa di Navigazione (A. Scinicariello, manager), Italy, and renamed NIRVO. *24.5.1943:* Bombed
and sunk during an air attack on Olbia. *1946:* Salved and returned to service under the ownership
of Angelo Scinicariello, Italy. *1952:* Sold to Franco Maresca, Italy, and renamed MAR GLAUCO.
8.1958: Sold to S.p.A. Cantieri Navali Santa Maria for demolition at La Spezia, Italy.

TREMORVAH

TRELISSICK   *W.S.S.-Marquis Collection*

78. TRELISSICK (II) (1919 — 1941)
O.N. 142567. 5265g, 3223n. 400.9 × 52.3 × 28.5 feet.
T. 3-cyl. by the Shipbuilder.
29.4.1919: Launched by Harland and Wolff Ltd., Glasgow (Yard No. 551), as WAR PAMPAS for
The Shipping Controller. Purchased and *6.1919* completed as TRELISSICK for The Hain
Steamship Co. Ltd. *23.6.1941:* Bombed and sunk by German aircraft $3\frac{1}{4}$ miles from Sheringham
Buoy, whilst on a voyage from London to the River Tyne and Pepel in ballast. Two of her crew
of 42 were lost.

TREVARRACK
J. Clarkson

79. TREVARRACK (III) (1919 — 1941)
O.N. 142568. 5270g, 3197n. 400.0 × 52.3 × 28.4 feet.
T. 3-cyl. by the Shipbuilder.
2.6.1919: Launched by D. and W. Henderson and Co. Ltd., Glasgow (Yard No. 519), as WAR LAUREL for The Shipping Controller. Purchased and *6.1919* completed as TREVARRACK for The Hain Steamship Co. Ltd. *29.12.1940:* Abandoned after an attack by German aircraft, N.W. of Tory Island, in a position 55.34 N, 09.30 W, whilst on a voyage from Durban to Immingham with a cargo of ore and carbides. *2.1.1941:* Towed to Rothesay Bay and 13.3.1941 bombed and sunk by German aircraft whilst under repair in Dalmuir Basin. *26.3.1941:* Refloated and subsequently repaired and returned to service. *8.6.1941:* Torpedoed and sunk by the German submarine U.46, in mid-Atlantic in a position 48.46 N, 29.14 W, whilst on a voyage from Glasgow to Montreal in ballast. Her crew of 37 and seven passengers were lost.

80. TREVELYAN (II) (1919 — 1923)
O.N. 142569. 2500g, 1456n. 303.0 × 43.0 × 20.8 feet.
T. 3-cyl. by Richardsons, Westgarth and Co. Ltd., Hartlepool.
1.5.1919: Launched by C. Hill and Son Ltd., Bristol (Yard No. 132), as WAR QUINCE for The Shipping Controller. Purchased and *7.1919* completed as TREVELYAN for The Hain Steamship Co. Ltd. *22.3.1923:* Sold for £24,000 to Kelvin Shipping Co. Ltd. (H. Hogarth and Sons, managers), Glasgow, and renamed BARON HERRIES. *1934:* Sold to Abbey Line Ltd. (Frederick Jones and Sons, managers), Cardiff, and renamed NEATH ABBEY. *1939:* Sold to Constants (South Wales) Ltd. (M. Constant, manager), Cardiff, and renamed LYMINGE. *1946:* Sold to Wheelock, Marden and Co. Ltd., London. *1947:* Sold to San Peh S.N. Co. Ltd., registered under Hoong On S.N. Co. Ltd., China, and renamed TUNG SHAN. *15.8.1949:* Bombed and sunk by Chinese Nationalist aircraft in the Yangtsze River 60 miles from Shanghai whilst on a voyage from Shanghai to Pukow in ballast.

TREVELYAN in Roath Dock, Cardiff, December 1920   *Welsh Industrial & Maritime Museum*

60

TREGENNA *W.S.S.-Marquis Collection*

81.   TREGENNA (IV) (1919 — 1940)
O.N. 142570. 5242g, 3201n. 400.1 × 52.3 × 28.4 feet.
T.3-cyl. by Central Marine Engine Works, West Hartlepool.
1.5.1919: Launched by Wm. Gray and Co. (1918) Ltd., West Hartlepool (Yard No. 915), as WAR BULLDOG for The Shipping Controller. Purchased and *7.1919* completed as TREGENNA for The Hain Steamship Co. Ltd. *17.9.1940:* Torpedoed and sunk by the German submarine U.65, N.W. of Rockall in a position 58.22 N, 15.42 W whilst on a voyage from Philadelphia to Newport, Mon. with a cargo of 8000 tons of steel. The vessel was sailing in convoy HX71 at the time of her sinking. 33 of her crew of 37 were lost.

82.   TRELYON (III) (1919 — 1938)
O.N. 142571. 5294g, 3232n. 400.0 × 52.4 × 28.5 feet.
T.3-cyl. by the Shipbuilder.
12.6.1919: Launched by J. Readhead and Sons Ltd., South Shields (Yard No. 11), as WAR PLOVER for The Shipping Controller. Purchased and *8.1919* completed as TRELYON for The Hain Steamship Co. Ltd. *1938:* Sold for £34,000 to Rickmers Rhederei A.G., Germany and renamed HANS RICKMERS. *30.11.1942:* Beached after striking a mine off Petsamo, Finland, and subsequently destroyed by Russian artillery.

TRELYON *V. Brownlie*

61

TRECARRELL   *Welsh Industrial & Maritime Museum*

83.   TRECARRELL (II) (1919 — 1941)
O.N. 142572. 5272g, 3198n. 400.1 × 52.3 × 28.4 feet.
T.3-cyl. by the Shipbuilder.
15.7.1919: Launched by D. and W. Henderson and Co. Ltd., Glasgow (Yard No. 520), as WAR
LILAC for The Shipping Controller. Purchased and *8.1919* completed as TRECARRELL for The Hain
Steamship Co. Ltd. *4.6.1941:* Torpedoed and sunk by the German submarine U.101, W. of Cape
Race in a position 47.10 N, 31.00 W whilst on a voyage from Hull to Father Point in the River
St. Lawrence in ballast. Four of her crew of 43 were lost.

TREVEAL wrecked on Kimmeridge Ledge, photographed from a passing
excursion steamer   *K. Ingram Collection*

84.   TREVEAL (II) (1919 — 1920)
O.N. 142573. 5243g, 3226n. 400.7 × 52.3 × 28.5 feet.
T.3-cyl. by the Shipbuilder.
11.6.1919: Launched by Harland and Wolff Ltd., Glasgow (Yard No. 549), as WAR JONQUIL for
The Shipping Controller. Purchased and *9.1919* completed as TREVEAL for The Hain Steamship
Co. Ltd. *9.1.1920:* Wrecked on Kimmeridge Ledge, 2 miles West of St. Alban's Head, whilst on
a voyage from Calcutta to Dundee with a cargo of jute and manganese ore. Earlier in the day the
ship had called at Portland for a pilot but none was available and the master was instructed to
continue the voyage.

62

TREMATON

A. Duncan

85. TREMATON (III) (1919 — 1937)
O.N. 142574. 5202g, 3179n. 400.1 × 52.3 × 28.4 feet.
T.3-cyl. by the Shipbuilder.
10.9.1919: Launched by D. and W. Henderson and Co. Ltd., Glasgow (Yard No. 521), as WAR LILY for The Shipping Controller. Purchased and *10.1919* completed as TREMATON for The Hain Steamship Co. Ltd. *1937:* Sold for £61,500 to Slobodna Plovidba Topić D.D. (Ant. Topić, manager), Yugoslavia, and renamed JURKO TOPIC. *1946:* Sold to Dubrovacka Plovidba A.D., Yugoslavia, and renamed KORENICA. *1947:* Taken over by State Enterprise Jugoslovenska Slobodna Plovidba, Yugoslavia. *1956:* Transferred to Atlantska Plovidba, Yugoslavia. *1960:* Sold to Japanese shipbreakers and *29.4.1960* arrived at Osaka. *14.5.1960:* Demolition commenced.

TREKIEVE arriving at Dunkirk from the River Plate

K. Ingram Collection

86. TREKIEVE (III) (1919 — 1942)
O.N. 142575. 5244g, 3230n. 400.0 × 52.4 × 28.5 feet.
T.3-cyl. by the Shipbuilder.
9.9.1919: Launched by J. Readhead and Sons Ltd., South Shields (Yard No. 12), as WAR MALLARD for The Shipping Controller. Purchased by *11.1919* completed as TREKIEVE for The Hain Steamship Co. Ltd. *4.11.1942:* Torpedoed and sunk by the German submarine U.178, E. of Lourenço Marques in a position 25.46 S, 33.48 E whilst on a voyage from Bombay and Mahe to Dúrban and the U.K. with a cargo of 2500 tons of manganese ore, 1700 tons of nuts and 1650 tons of copra and general cargo. 3 crew were lost.

63

TREFUSIS   *Welsh Industrial & Maritime Museum*

87.   TREFUSIS (II) (1919 — 1943)
O.N. 142634. 5299g, 3229n. 400.3 × 52.4 × 28.5 feet.
T.3-cyl. by Harland and Wolff Ltd., Glasgow.
27.7.1918: Launched by Wm. Doxford and Sons Ltd., Sunderland (Yard No. 529), as WAR ACONITE for The Shipping Controller (W. Runciman and Co. Ltd., managers). *10.1919:* Completed *1919:* Purchased by The Hain Steamship Co. Ltd. and renamed TREFUSIS. *5.3.1943:* Torpedoed and sunk by the German submarine U.130, W. of Cape Finisterre in a position 43.50 N, 14.46 W whilst on a voyage from Pepel to London with a cargo of 7400 tons of iron ore. The ship was sailing in Convoy XK2 at the time of the sinking. 3 crew were lost.

TREGONNELL   *A. Duncan*

88.   TREGONNELL (1919 — 1935)
O.N. 142431. 5249g, 3178n. 400.0 × 52.3 × 28.5 feet.
T.3-cyl. by the Shipbuilder.
28.3.1918: Launched by Wm. Doxford and Sons Ltd., Sunderland (Yard No. 525), as WAR STAG for The Shipping Controller (Watts, Watts and Co. Ltd., managers). *1918:* Completed. *1919:* Purchased by The Hain Steamship Co. Ltd. and renamed TREGONNELL. *1935:* Sold for £15,650 to A. Lauro, Italy and renamed IRIS. *25.6.1943:* Bombed and sunk during an air attack on Messina. *4.1947:* Raised after 8 months work and on 21.5.1947 left in tow for Spezia for repair. 1948: Recommissioned. *1958:* Sold to Cantieri "Tomaso di Savoia" for demolition and 10.4.1958 arrived at Spezia.

89.   TREVERBYN (II) (1920 — 1941)
O.N. 142576. 5281g, 3294n. 400.7 × 52.3 × 28.5 feet.
T.3-cyl. by the Shipbuilder.
22.11.1919: Launched by Harland and Wolff Ltd., Glasgow (Yard No. 530), as WAR AIRMAN for
The Shipping Controller (having been laid down as WAR MAPLE). Purchased and *1.1920*
completed as TREVERBYN for The Hain Steamship Co. Ltd. *21.10.1941:* Torpedoed and sunk by
the German submarine U.82, S.W. of Cape Clear, in a position approximately 51 N, 19 W. She
was on a voyage from Pepel to Cardiff with a cargo of 6900 tons of iron ore. The ship was sailing
in Convoy SL.89 at the time of the sinking. Her crew of 38 and 10 gunners were lost.

TREVERBYN   *Welsh Industrial & Maritime Museum*

TREWYN   *Warwick Foote*

90.   TREWYN (II) (1920 — 1937)
O.N. 142577. 5241g, 3228n. 400.1 × 52.4 × 28.5 feet.
T.3-cyl. by the Shipbuilder.
8.12.1919: Launched by J. Readhead and Sons Ltd., South Shields (Yard No. 13), as WAR
GANNET for The Shipping Controller. Purchased and *2.1920* completed as TREWYN for The Hain
Steamship Co. Ltd. *1937:* Sold to for £61,800 Rickmers Rhederei A.G., Germany and renamed
MONI RICKMERS. *10.5.1940:* Seized at Sabang by Dutch authorities, renamed SALANDO and

operated by the Dutch Government (N.V. Nederlandsch-Indische Maats. voor Zeevaart VI.) *1943:* Management transferred to Netherlands Shipping and Trading Co. Ltd. *1945:* Management transferred to Rotterdamsche Lloyd. *1948:* Management transferred to A. Veder and Co. *1949:* Sold to Avni Nuri Meserretcioglu, Turkey and renamed MESERRET. *1958:* Sold to A. Veder, Holland. *1959:* Sold to Hakki Marmara, Turkey and renamed YENI MESERRET. *1960:* Sold to Deniz Nakliyat ve Ticaret Limited Sirketi, Turkey. *1.9.1962:* Driven ashore at Green Island, Hong Kong during typhoon "Wanda". *6.9.1962:* Refloated and beached at Gin Drinker's Bay where she was broken up by Hong Kong Chiap Hua Manufactory Co. (1947) Ltd. *24.9.1962:* Demolition commenced.

TREVORIAN   *Welsh Industrial & Maritime Museum*

91.   TREVORIAN (III) (1920 — 1943)
O.N. 142578. 4599g, 2845n. 400.3 × 52.1 × 25.9 feet.
T.3-cyl. by the Shipbuilder.
1.6.1920: Launched by J. Readhead and Sons Ltd., South Shields (Yard No. 462), for The Hain Steamship Co. Ltd. *10.1920:* Completed. *28.11.1943:* Sank in the North Sea following a collision with the Icelandic trawler OLI GARDA 316/21, whilst on a voyage from Hull to Mediterranean ports.

TREBARTHA

92.   TREBARTHA (I) (1920 — 1940)
O.N. 142579. 4597g, 2847n. 400.1 × 52.1 × 25.9 feet.
T.3-cyl. by the Shipbuilder.
31.8.1920: Launched by J. Readhead and Sons Ltd., South Shields (Yard No. 463), for The Hain Steamship Co. Ltd. *12.1920:* Completed. *11.11.1940:* Bombed by German aircraft 4 miles S.E. of Aberdeen whilst on a voyage from London to Philadelphia in ballast. On fire forward and run ashore in Cove Bay, Kincardineshire, 3 miles S. of Aberdeen. She broke in two *15.11.1940* and was abandoned as a total loss. 4 crew were lost.

93.   TREVESSA (II) (1920 — 1923)
O.N. 143920. 5004g, 3121n. 401.2 × 52.7 × 28.3 feet.
Q.4-cyl. by the Shipbuilder.
25.8.1909: Launched by Flensburger Schiffsbau-Gesellschaft, Flensburg (Yard No. 290), as
IMKENTURM for Deutsche Dampfschifffahrts Gesellschaft Hansa, Germany. *10.1909:* Completed.
1919: Surrendered to Great Britain as a prize and allocated to The Shipping Controller (British
India S.N. Co. Ltd., managers). *19.10.1920:* Purchased for £86,000 by The Hain Steamship Co.
Ltd., and renamed TREVESSA. *4.6.1923:* Foundered in the Indian Ocean whilst on a voyage from
Port Pirie and Fremantle to the U.K. and Antwerp with a cargo of zinc concentrates.

TREVESSA   *St. Ives Museum*

TRELEVAN

94.   TRELEVAN (I) (1920 — 1929)
O.N. 144396. 4770g, 2937n. 396.5 × 54.8 × 26.2 feet.
T.3-cyl. by the Shipbuilder.
17.4.1914: Launched by Flensburger Schiffsbau-Gesellschaft, Flensburg, (Yard No. 338), as
LUBECK for Deutsch-Australische D.G., Germany. *6.1914:* Completed *1919:* Surrendered to
Great Britain as a prize and allocated to The Shipping Controller (British India S.N. Co. Ltd.,
managers). *18.11.1920:* Purchased for £121,350 by The Hain Steamship Co. Ltd. and renamed
TRELEVAN. *1929:* Sold to Donaldson Line Ltd. (Donaldson Bros. and Co. Ltd., managers), Glasgow
and renamed AIRTHRIA. *1938:* Sold to Rederi A/B Atlanta (B. Krogius, manager), Finland and
renamed ANJA. *1941:* Taken over by the United States Maritime Commission, registered under
the Panamanian flag and renamed SCAPA FLOW. *14.11.1942:* Torpedoed and sunk by the
German submarine U.134, S.W. of Cape Verde Island whilst on a voyage from W. African ports
to Baltimore. She carried a cargo of 4500 tons of manganese ore, 1500 tons of latex in drums
and 500 tons of baled rubber. 33 of her crew were lost.

TREDINNICK *Welsh Industrial & Maritime Museum*

95. TREDINNICK (1920 — 1942)
O.N. 142580. 4597g, 2846n. 400.1 × 52.1 × 25.9 feet.
T.3-cyl. by the Shipbuilder.
25.11.1920: Launched by J. Readhead and Sons Ltd., South Shields (Yard No. 464), for The Hain Steamship Co. Ltd. *2.1921:* Completed. *29.3.1942:* Torpedoed and sunk by the Italian submarine CALVI, S.E. of Bermuda in a position 27.15 N, 49.15 W whilst on a voyage from New York to Bombay via Table Bay with a cargo of Government stores and general. Her crew of 46, including 6 gunners was lost.

96. TREDENHAM (1920 — 1924)
O.N. 143074. 8435g, 5369n. 479.7 × 62.2 × 33.0 feet.
Q.4-cyl. by the Shipbuilder.
1915: Completed by A. G. "Weser", Bremen (Yard No. 208), as FALKENFELS for Deutsche Dampfschifffahrts Gesellschaft Hansa, Germany. *1919:* Surrendered to Great Britain as a prize and allocated to The Shipping Controller (James Chambers and Co., managers). *9.12.1920:* Purchased for £190,000 by The Hain Steamship Co. Ltd. and renamed TREDENHAM. *1924:* Sold to Federal Steam Navigation Co. Ltd., London and renamed PAREORA. *1934:* Sold to Japanese shipbreakers and 7.4.1934 arrived at Tokuyama to be broken up.

TREDENHAM *D. N. Brigham Collection*

68

TREMERE   *V. Brownlie*

97. TREMERE (1920 — 1924)
O.N. 143094. 8047g, 5038n. 475.6 × 60.9 × 33.0 feet.
T.3-cyl. by the Shipbuilder.
22.1.1915: Launched by Flensburger Schiffsbau-Gesellschaft, Flensburg (Yard No. 343), as AUGSBURG for Norddeutscher Lloyd, Germany. *2.1916:* Completed. *1919:* Surrendered to Great Britain as a prize and allocated to The Shipping Controller (Watts, Watts and Co. Ltd., managers). *9.12.1920:* Purchased for £180,000 by The Hain Steamship Co. Ltd. and renamed TREMERE. *1924:* Sold to Federal Steam Navigation Co. Ltd., London and renamed PURIRI. *1934:* Sold to Japanese shipbreakers.

98. TREVITHICK (1920 — 1924)
O.N. 144525. 8046g, 5128n. 469.8 × 58.1 × 32.1 feet.
Q.4-cyl. by the Shipbuilder.
1910: Launched by John Brown and Co. Ltd., Clydebank (Yard No. 417), as PREUSSEN for Hamburg-Amerikanische Packetfahrt A.G., Germany. *12.1910:* Completed. *1919:* Surrendered to Great Britain as a prize and allocated to The Shipping Controller (British India S.N. Co. Ltd., managers). *13.12.1920:* Purchased for £160,000 by The Hain Steamship Co. Ltd. and renamed TREVITHICK. *1924:* Sold to Federal Steam Navigation Co. Ltd., London and renamed PAPANUI. *1934:* Sold to Japanese shipbreakers, and *14.3.1934* sailed from Shimonoseki bound for Kuchinotsu.

TREVITHICK   *K. Ingram Collection*

TREWINNARD   *W.S.S.-Marquis Collection*

99. TREWINNARD (1920 — 1924)
O.N. 143291. 7233g, 4448n. 472.0 × 60.9 × 28.6 feet.
T.3-cyl. by the Shipbuilder.
16.5.1914: Launched by Flensburger Schiffsbau-Gesellschaft, Flensburg (Yard No. 339), as AMMON for Deutsche Dampfschifffahrts Gesellschaft Kosmos, Germany. *7.1914:* Completed.
1919: Surrendered to Great Britain as a prize and allocated to The Shipping Controller (Glover Brothers, managers). *13.12.1920:* Purchased for £170,000 by The Hain Steamship Co. Ltd. and renamed TREWINNARD. *1924:* Sold to Federal Steam Navigation Co. Ltd., London and renamed PAKIPAKI. *1933:* Sold to Italian shipbreakers.

TRESITHNEY

100. TRESITHNEY (1921 — 1924)
O.N. 143148. 6714g, 4162n. 472.5 × 59.3 × 28.6 feet.
T.3-cyl. by the Shipbuilder.
8.8.1914: Launched by Flensburger Schiffsbau-Gesellschaft, Flensburg (Yard No. 341), as LIPPE for Norddeutscher Lloyd, Germany. *2.1915:* Completed. *1919:* Surrendered to Great Britain as a prize and allocated to The Shipping Controller (Cairns, Noble and Co., managers). *1.2.1921:* Purchased for £120,000 by The Hain Steamship Co. Ltd., and renamed TRESITHNEY. *1924:* Sold to Federal Steam Navigation Co. Ltd., London and renamed PIPIRIKI. *1933:* Sold to Italian shipbreakers.

TREWORLAS

101. TREWORLAS (I) (1922 — 1942)
O.N. 147041. 4692g, 2898n. 400.4 × 53.1 × 26.3 feet.
T.3-cyl. by the Shipbuilder.
5.10.1922: Launched by J. Readhead and Sons Ltd., South Shields (Yard No. 470), for The Hain Steamship Co. Ltd. *11.1922:* Completed. *28.12.1942:* Torpedoed and sunk by the German submarine U.124, E. of Trinidad in a position 10.52 N, 60.45 W whilst on a voyage from Massowah to Baltimore with 3000 tons of manganese ore. 33 crew and 5 gunners were lost.

TREMINNARD

102. MIN (II)/TREMINNARD (1923 — 1942)
O.N. 142582. 4694g, 2901n. 400.4 × 53.1 × 26.3 feet.
T.3-cyl. by the Shipbuilder.
25.5.1922: Launched by J. Readhead and Sons Ltd., South Shields (Yard No. 469), as MIN for Mercantile Steam Ship Co. Ltd. (E. Hain and Son, managers), St. Ives. *7.1922:* Completed. *8.11.1923:* Transferred to The Hain Steamship Co. Ltd. *1936:* Renamed TREMINNARD. *2.8.1942:* Torpedoed and sunk by the German submarine U.160, S.E. of Barbados in a position 10.40 N, 57.07 W whilst on a voyage from Alexandria to Trinidad and Ciudad Trujillo via Durban in ballast. The crew of 47 was rescued.

BOYNE

103. BOYNE (1923 — 1930)
O.N. 129121. 4445g, 2781n. 373.7 × 51.5 × 26.2 feet.
T.3-cyl. by Blair and Co. Ltd., Stockton on Tees.
18.6.1910: Launched by J. L. Thompson and Sons Ltd., Sunderland (Yard No. 473), as BOYNE for Mercantile Steam Ship Co. Ltd., London. *8.1910:* Completed. *1917:* E. Hain and Son appointed managers. *8.11.1923:* Transferred to The Hain Steamship Co. Ltd. *1930:* Sold for £22,400 to Marmara Steamship Co. Ltd., Greece and renamed ARIADNE PANDELIS. *19.6.1936:* Beached on fire at Itaparica, Brazil, and abandoned as a total loss. She was on a voyage from Gdynia to Mar del Plata.

FOYLE

104. FOYLE (1923 — 1934)
O.N. 139093. 4739g, 2952n. 400.0 × 53.0 × 26.0 feet.
T.3-cyl. by Blair and Co. Ltd., Stockton on Tees.
29.6.1915: Launched by J. L. Thompson and Sons Ltd., Sunderland (Yard No. 510), as FOYLE for Mercantile Steam Ship Co. Ltd., London. *10.1915:* Completed. *1917:* E. Hain and Son appointed managers. *8.11.1923:* Transferred to The Hain Steamship Co. Ltd. *1934:* Sold for £9,750 to Rethymnis & Kulukundis (Hellas) Ltd., and D. E. and M. Lemos (Rethymnis & Kulukundis Ltd., managers), Greece and renamed DELPHOI. *1936:* Owners restyled D. P., M. G. & E. P. Lemos and Rethymnis & Kulukundis (Hellas) Ltd. *9.11.1938:* Stranded at Chekka, Syria, whilst on a voyage from Gdynia to Chekka with a cargo of coal. Refloated and reported sold to Italian shipbreakers who resold her to F. A. Bertorello, Italy, who renamed her VOLODDA. Repaired and returned to service. *9.1943:* Scuttled at Bari. *1947:* Salved, repaired and returned to service. *1958:* Owners restyled as Febo Amedeo Bertorello fu Giacomo. *1960:* Sold to British Iron and Steel Corporation, allocated to P. and W. McLellan Ltd., and *10.8.1960* arrived at Bo'ness. *1.11.1960:* Demolition commenced.

PRUTH   *K. Ingram Collection*

105.   PRUTH (1923)
O.N. 139109. 4698g, 2945n. 400.0 × 53.0 × 26.0 feet.
T.3-cyl. by Blair and Co. Ltd., Stockton on Tees.
23.9.1915: Launched by J. L. Thompson and Sons Ltd., Sunderland (Yard No. 511), as PRUTH for Mercantile Steam Ship Co. Ltd., London. *1.1916:* Completed. *1917:* E. Hain and Son appointed managers. *8.11.1923:* Transferred to The Hain Steamship Co. Ltd. *31.12.1923:* Wrecked on Natara Reef, Port Moresby whilst on a voyage from New York to New Zealand ports via Samarai and Port Moresby with general cargo.

TRESILLIAN   *P&O Archives*

106.   TRESILLIAN (III) (1925 — 1941)
O.N. 148685. 4743g, 2873n. 400.0 × 53.0 × 26.4 feet.
T.3-cyl. by Central Marine Engine Works, West Hartlepool.
21.8.1925: Launched by Wm. Gray and Co. Ltd., West Hartlepool (Yard No. 968), for The Hain Steamship Co. Ltd. *10.1925:* Completed. *13.6.1941:*Torpedoed and sunk by the German submarine U.77, S.E. of Cape Race in a position 44.40 N, 45.30 W whilst on a voyage from Immingham to the River St. Lawrence in ballast. The crew of 46 was rescued.

TRELAWNY

P&O Archives

107. TRELAWNY (III) (1927 — 1941)
O.N. 149899. 4689g, 2876n. 406.0 × 54.7 × 25.2 feet.
T.3-cyl. by the Shipbuilder.
15.8.1927: Launched by Hawthorn, Leslie and Co. Ltd., Newcastle (Yard No. 546), for The Hain Steamship Co. Ltd. *9.1927:* Completed. *22.2.1941:* Sunk W. of the Seychelles, in a position 47.12 N, 40.13 W whilst on a voyage from Swansea to New York when the convoy was attacked by the German battleships SCHARNHORST and GNEISENAU. One of the crew of 40 was killed and the remainder taken prisoners of war.

108. NIMODA/TREMODA (1927 — 1941)
O.N. 149980. 4736g, 2858n. 409.0 × 55.8 × 25.0 feet.
T.3-cyl. by Harland and Wolff Ltd., Belfast.
24.11.1927: Launched by Harland and Wolff Ltd., Greenock (Yard No. 797), for The Hain Steamship Co. Ltd. *1.1928:* Completed. *1937:* Renamed TREMODA. *27.8.1941:* Torpedoed by the German submarine U.557, W. of Achill Island in a position 53.36 N, 16.40 W whilst on a voyage from London to Duala via the River Tyne with general cargo and war stores. The ship was sailing in Convoy OS.4 at the time of the attack and was last seen in a position 54.08 N, 15.28 W on the following day. 26 crew and 6 gunners were lost.

NIMODA

TREMODA

NOHATA *W. Foote*

109. NOHATA/TREHATA (1927 — 1942)
O.N. 149988. 4817g, 2862n. 413.2 x 54.2 x 25.1 feet.
T.3-cyl. by Central Marine Engine Works, West Hartlepool.
6.12.1927: Launched by Wm. Gray and Co. Ltd., West Hartlepool (Yard No. 994), for The Hain
Steamship Co. Ltd. *1.1928:* Completed. *1936:* Renamed TREHATA. *8.8.1942:* Torpedoed and
sunk by the German submarine U.176, S.E. of Cape Farewell in a position 56.30 N, 32.14 W. She
was on a voyage from Hampton Roads to Manchester with 3000 tons of steel, 1000 tons of tinned
goods, 1000 tons of lard, 1000 tons of cheese and 1000 tons of manufactured goods. 31 crew
were lost.

TREHATA *D. N. Brigham*

BANGALORE   *P&O Archives*

110.   BANGALORE (1928 — 1941)
O.N. 160547. 6067g, 2908n. 436.0 × 57.5 × 29.8 feet.
Q.4-cyl. by the Shipbuilder, with low pressure steam turbine.
5.6.1928: Launched by Barclay, Curle and Co. Ltd., Glasgow (Yard No. 622), for The Hain Steamship Co. Ltd. *8.1928:* Completed. *20.7.1941:* Damaged in collision with the British motorship RICHMOND CASTLE 7798/39 in a position 01.30 N, 41.54 W whilst on a voyage from London via Trinidad and Table Bay to Hong Kong with general cargo, aeroplanes and horses. *21.7.1941:* Sunk by gunfire of an escort ship in a position 00.59 N, 43.00 W to prevent her becoming a hazard to navigation.

BURDWAN in the River Thames, 2nd April 1938   *K. Ingram Collection*

111.   BURDWAN (1928 — 1942)
O.N. 160559. 6069g, 2911n. 436.0 × 57.5 × 29.8 feet.
Q. 4-cyl. by the Shipbuilder, with low pressure steam turbine.
5.7.1928: Launched by Barclay, Curle and Co. Ltd., Glasgow (Yard No. 623), for The Hain Steamship Co. Ltd. *9.1928:* Completed. *15.6.1942:* Bombed and severely damaged by German aircraft 35 miles S. of Pantellaria Island when on a voyage from Greenock and Gibraltar to Malta with a cargo of Government stores including ammunition and petrol. Abandoned by her crew, she was sunk by escorting warships. She carried a crew of 125 including military personnel; three were lost.

BEHAR *P&O Archives*

112. BEHAR (I) (1928 — 1940)

O.N. 160577. 6100g, 2942n. 436.0 × 57.6 × 29.6 feet.
Q. 4-cyl. by Harland and Wolff Ltd., Glasgow, with low pressure steam turbine.
16.8.1928: Launched by Harland and Wolff Ltd., Greenock (Yard No. 830), for The Hain Steamship Co. Ltd. *11.1928:* Completed. *24.11.1940:* Mined and badly damaged in a position 51.42 N, 05.07 W, when leaving Milford Haven with a cargo of 4770 tons of Government stores. Subsequently beached 230° from Great Castle Head Lower Light and declared a constructive total loss. The crew of 71 was rescued. Salvage efforts continued, but were hindered by the weather and enemy minelaying. Work was eventually abandoned and *27.10.1941* the wreck was sold to British Iron and Steel Corporation (Salvage) Ltd. for demolition "in situ".

BHUTAN, 7th March 1936 *John G. Callis*

113. BHUTAN (1928 — 1942)

O.N. 161203. 6104g, 2943n. 436.0 × 57.6 × 29.6 feet.
Q. 4-cyl. by the Shipbuilder, with low pressure steam turbine.
12.12.1928: Launched by Harland and Wolff Ltd., Glasgow (Yard No. 842), for The Hain Steamship Co. Ltd. *3.1929:* Completed. *14.6.1942:* Bombed and sunk by enemy aircraft S. of Pantellaria Island in a position 34.00 N, 23.40 E, whilst on a voyage from Alexandria to Malta. The ship was sailing in a convoy which had been under continuous air attack since leaving Alexandria three days previously. She carried a cargo of 7500 tons of Government stores including high explosives, aviation spirit and food. Six were lost from her crew of 128, 28 gunners and 52 passengers.

77

114. SOMALI (1930)

O.N. 161938. 6809g, 3550n. 459.0 × 60.7 × 29.7 feet.
Q. 4-cyl. by J. G. Kincaid and Co. Ltd., Greenock, with low pressure steam turbine.
9.10.1930: Launched by Harland and Wolff Ltd., Glasgow (Yard No. 898), for The Hain Steamship Co. Ltd. Sold whilst fitting out to Peninsular and Oriental Steam Navigation Company and *18.12.1930* delivered. *26.3.1941:* Bombed by German aircraft off the Northumberland coast and hit by three bombs in her No.3 hold. Her cargo of straw, hay, paint and oil was ignited and was soon blazing out of control. The crew was evacuated and on *27.3.1941* she blew up and sank 1 mile E. of Snoop Head, Sunderland.

TREWELLARD   *P&O Archives*

115. TREWELLARD (III) (1936 — 1940)

O.N. 164680. 5201g, 3067n. 432.3 × 56.2 × 24.8 feet.
T. 3-cyl. by D. Rowan and Co. Ltd., Glasgow.
16.6.1936: Launched by Lithgows Ltd., Port Glasgow (Yard No. 883), for The Hain Steamship Co. Ltd. *7.1936:* Completed. *5.11.1940:* Shelled and sunk by the German raider ADMIRAL SCHEER, S.E. of Greenland, in an approximate position 52.26 N, 32.34 W. She was on a voyage from Boston and Halifax N.S. to Liverpool with 7800 tons of steel and 12 aeroplanes. 16 crew were lost.

TREGARTHEN   *W. Foote*

116. TREGARTHEN (III) (1936 — 1941)

O.N. 164706. 5201g, 3067n. 432.3 × 56.2 × 24.8 feet.
T. 3-cyl. by D. Rowan and Co. Ltd., Glasgow.
30.7.1936: Launched by Lithgows Ltd., Port Glasgow (Yard No. 884), for The Hain Steamship Co. Ltd. *9.1936:* Completed. *6.6.1941:* Torpedoed and sunk by the German submarine U.48, W. of Cape Race, in position 46.17 N, 36.20 W. She was on a voyage from Cardiff to Kingston, Jamaica, with 7800 tons of coal. Her crew of 59 were lost.

117. TREVALGAN (III) (1937 — 1942)
O.N. 165560. 5299g, 3120n. 432.3 × 56.2 × 24.8 feet.
3-cyl. 2 S.C.S.A. Doxford oil engine by Barclay, Curle and Co. Ltd., Glasgow.
29.6.1937: Launched by Lithgows Ltd., Port Glasgow (Yard No. 898), for The Hain Steamship
Co. Ltd. *8.1937:* Completed. *30.11.1942:* Torpedoed by the German submarine U.508 and sank
2.12.1942 S.E. of Trinidad, in position 09.40 N, 59.15 W. She was on a voyage from Suez and
Table Bay to Trinidad and New York in ballast. Her crew of 43 was rescued.

TREVALGAN

TREVANION   *Welsh Industrial & Maritime Museum*

118. TREVANION (III) (1937 — 1939)
O.N. 165602. 5299g, 3120n. 432.3 × 56.2 × 24.8 feet.
3-cyl. 2 S.C.S.A. Doxford oil engine by Barclay, Curle and Co. Ltd., Glasgow.
9.9.1937: Launched by Lithgows Ltd., Port Glasgow (Yard No. 899), for The Hain Steamship Co.
Ltd. *11.1937:* Completed. *22.10.1939:* Intercepted by the German pocket battleship ADMIRAL
GRAF SPEE in the South Atlantic in position 19.40 S, 04.02 E. After removal of the crew, she
was sunk with time bombs. She was on a voyage from Port Pirie and Fremantle to Table Bay
and Swansea with a cargo of concentrates.

TREVAYLOR   *Welsh Industrial & Maritime Museum*

119 TREVAYLOR (III) (1940 — 1955)
O.N. 167400. 5257g, 3091n. 432.5 (447.8 o.l.) × 56.2 × 24.9 feet.
3-cyl. 2 S.C.S.A. Doxford oil engine by the Shipbuilder.
9.1.1940: Launched by Barclay, Curle and Co. Ltd., Glasgow (Yard No. 674), for The Hain Steamship Co. Ltd. *3.1940:* Completed. *1955:* Sold to Williamson and Co. Ltd., Hong Kong, and renamed INCHSTAFFA. *1966:* Sold to Rowan Shipping Corporation Ltd., Hong Kong. Resold to Mullion and Co. Ltd., Gibraltar, and renamed ARDSTAFFA. *1967:* Sold to Southern Shipping and Enterprises Co. Ltd., Hong Kong, and renamed NANKWANG. *30.11.1967:* Stranded and sank off Woosung anchorage after breaking her anchor chain in heavy weather. She was on a voyage from Whampoa to Shanghai with a cargo of ore.

120. TREVETHOE (III) (1940 — 1941)
O.N. 167555. 5257g, 3083n. 432.5 (446.7 o.l.) × 56.2 × 24.9 feet.
3-cyl. 2 S.C.S.A. Doxford oil engine by Barclay, Curle and Co. Ltd., Glasgow.
10.4.1940: Launched by A. Stephen and Sons Ltd., Glasgow (Yard No. 570), for The Hain Steamship Co. Ltd. *6.1940:* Completed. *11.3.1941:* Torpedoed and sunk by German E-boat N.E. of Yarmouth, in position 52.46 N, 01.57 E. She was on a voyage from St. John N.B. to London with 8160 tons of wheat. One of her crew of 38 was lost.

121. TREVILLEY (IV) (1940 — 1942)
O.N. 167621. 5296g, 3106n. 431.9 (448.5 o.l.) × 56.2 × 24.8 feet.
3-cyl. 2 S.C.S.A. Doxford oil engine by Barclay, Curle and Co. Ltd., Glasgow.
24.4.1940: Launched by Lithgows Ltd., Port Glasgow (Yard No. 928), for The Hain Steamship Co. Ltd. *8.1940:* Completed. *12.9.1942:* Torpedoed, shelled and sunk by the German submarine U.68 in the South Atlantic in position 04.30 S, 07.50 W. She was on a voyage from Middlesbrough and Oban to Table Bay and Beira with 6000 tons of general cargo and military stores.

TREVILLEY   *K. Ingram Collection*

TREVELYAN

122. TREVELYAN (III) (1943 — 1956)(1958 — 1962)
O.N. 168475. 7292g, 4970n. 428.8 (442.9 o.l.) × 56.5 × 35.5 feet.
3-cyl. 2 S.C.S.A. oil engine by the Shipbuilder.
8.4.1943: Launched by W. Doxford and Sons Ltd., Sunderland (Yard No. 704), for The Hain Steamship Co. Ltd. *7.1943:* Completed. *1956:* Transferred to P. and O. Steam Navigation Company. *1958:* Returned to The Hain Steamship Co. Ltd. *20.10.1962:* Sold for £52,000 to Sigma Shipping Co. Ltd. for demolition and work commenced *5.11.1962* at Hong Kong.

123. BEHAR (II) (1943 — 1944)
O.N. 168497. 7840g, 3864n. 465.7 (485.5 o.l.) × 62.9 × 38.3 feet.
Two 4-cyl. 2 S.C.S.A. Doxford oil engines by the Shipbuilder.
24.5.1943: Launched by Barclay, Curle and Co. Ltd., Glasgow (Yard No. 692), for The Hain Steamship Co. Ltd. *8.1943:* Completed. *9.3.1944:* Shelled and sunk by the Japanese cruiser TONE, S.W. of the Cocos Islands in position 20.32 S, 87.10 E. She was on a voyage from Newcastle N.S.W. and Melbourne to Bombay with a cargo of 796 tons of zinc. She carried a crew of 90, 20 gunners and nine passengers. Three crew were killed during the action and the remainder were taken aboard the cruiser. Of these, 71 were executed by the Japanese on *18.3.1944* and others subsequently died in prisoner of war camps.

BEHAR   *P&O Archives*

TREVINCE

124. TREVINCE (II) (1943 — 1959)
O.N. 169571. 7292g, 4969n. 428.8 (442.9 o.l.) × 56.5 × 35.5 feet.
3-cyl. 2 S.C.S.A. oil engine by the Shipbuilder.
4.5.1943: Launched by W. Doxford and Sons Ltd., Sunderland (Yard No. 705), for The Hain Steamship Co. Ltd. *8.1943:* Completed. *23.9.1959:* Sold for £135,000 to Black Star Line Ltd., Ghana, and renamed DENSU RIVER. *1967:* Sold to Compania de Naviera Victoria S.A., Panama, and renamed VICKY. *1973:* Sold to Holivian Shipping Co. S.A., Panama. *4.6.1974:* Arrived in tow at Saigon, Vietnam, after her engines had broken down during a voyage from Penang. Repairs were considered uneconomical and she was towed to Hong Kong. After minor repairs she sailed *24.7.1974* for Whampoa for demolition by Chinese shipbreakers. *27.7.1974:* Delivered at Whampoa.

TREVANION   *D. N. Brigham*

125. TREVANION (IV) (1943 — 1955)
O.N. 169710. 7375g, 5134n. 432.6 (447.2 o.l.) × 57.9 × 35.3 feet.
6-cyl. 4 S.C.S.A. Burmeister & Wain oil engine by Harland and Wolff Ltd., Glasgow.
11.11.1943: Launched by Lithgows Ltd., Port Glasgow (Yard No. 985), for The Hain Steamship Co. Ltd. *1.1944:* Completed. *25.4.1955:* Sold to The Aviation and Shipping Co. Ltd. (N. W. Purvis, manager), London, and renamed AVISBROOK. *1957:* Purvis Shipping Co. Ltd. appointed managers. *1960:* Sold to Integritas Shipping Co. Ltd., Greece, and renamed MICHALIS. *1967:* Sold to Taiwan shipbreakers and arrived *23.10.1967* at Kaohsiung.

126. HARDINGHAM (1944 — 1945)
O.N. 168314. 7269g, 5041n. 428.8 (442.9 o.l.) × 56.5 × 35.5 feet.
3-cyl. 2 S.C.S.A. oil engine by the Shipbuilder.
1.6.1942: Launched by W. Doxford and Sons Ltd., Sunderland (Yard No. 692), as HARDINGHAM for Willis Steamship Co. Ltd. (J. and C. Harrison Ltd., managers), London. *9.1942:* Completed. *1944:* Purchased by The Hain Steamship Co. Ltd. *5.4.1945:* Lost by fire and explosion in the Outer Anchorage, near Colombo, whilst on a voyage from New York to Calcutta with general cargo including explosives.

TREWIDDEN   *Skyfotos*

127. HARLESDEN/TREWIDDEN (IV) (1944 — 1959)
O.N. 168406. 7273g, 4984n. 428.8 (442.9 o.l.) × 56.5 × 35.5 feet.
3-cyl. 2 S.C.S.A. oil engine by the Shipbuilder.
23.10.1942: Launched by W. Doxford and Sons Ltd., Sunderland (Yard No. 699), as HARLESDEN, for J. and C. Harrison Ltd., London. *3.1943:* Completed. *1944:* Purchased by The Hain Steamship Co. Ltd. *1945:* Renamed TREWIDDEN. *20.4.1959:* Sold for £142,000 to Black Star Line Ltd., Ghana, and renamed ANKOBRA RIVER. *1964:* Sold to Tenes Shipping Company, Liberia, and renamed ELAND. *1968:* Sold to Tien Cheng Steel Manufacturing Ltd. for demolition and arrived *29.10.1968* at Kaohsiung, Taiwan.

TREWELLARD   *Skyfotos*

128. HARPALYCE/TREWELLARD (IV) (1944 — 1956) (1958 — 1962)
O.N. 168334. 7269g, 5042n. 428.8 (442.9 o.l.) × 56.5 × 35.5 feet.
3-cyl. 2 S.C.S.A. oil engine by the Shipbuilder.
30.6.1942: Launched by W. Doxford and Sons Ltd., Sunderland (Yard No. 694), as HARPALYCE for National Steamship Co. Ltd. (J. and C. Harrison Ltd., managers), London. *10.1942:* Completed. *1944:* Purchased by The Hain Steamship Co. Ltd. *1946:* Renamed TREWELLARD. *1956:* Transferred to P. and O. Steam Navigation Company. *1958:* Returned to The Hain Steamship Co. Ltd. *12.10.1962:* Sold for £70,000 to Santa Marina Compania Maritima S.A., Greece, and renamed ARTEMON. *7.10.1965:* Arrived at Piraeus, Greece, with engine trouble sustained whilst on a voyage from Cebu to Rotterdam. Fire broke out in her cargo, and was discovered *1.11.1965,* and as a result she was beached in Ambelaki Bay in order that fire fighting could take place. The fire was not extinguished until *8.11.1965.* Declared a constructive total loss and left Piraeus in tow *29.9.1966* for Valencia and demolition. *12.1966:* Work commenced by Desguaces Incolesa.

The after-part of **HARPAGUS** at Southampton following discharge
13th September 1944   *K. Ingram Collection*

HARPAGUS at Southampton   *K. Ingram Collection*

129.   HARPAGUS/TREWORLAS (II) (1944 — 1956) (1958 — 1960)
O.N. 168347. 7271g, 5044n. 428.8 (442.9 o.l.) × 56.5 × 35.5 feet.
3-cyl. 2 S.C.S.A. oil engine by the Shipbuilder.
28.8.1942: Launched by W. Doxford and Sons Ltd., Sunderland (Yard No. 695), as HARPAGUS
for National Steamship Co. Ltd. (J. and C. Harrison Ltd., managers), London. *11.1942:* Completed.
1944: Purchased by The Hain Steamship Co. Ltd. *19.8.1944:* Struck a mine 1¼ miles North of
the West Breakwater, Arromanches Harbour, France, whilst on a voyage from Southend to
Arromanches with a cargo of military stores. She broke in two, and the fore-part quickly sank.
The after-part was beached, but later refloated and towed to Southampton for discharge. She
was taken in tow for the River Tyne, but grounded again on West Barrow Sand in the Thames

84

HARPAGUS at Southampton
K. Ingram Collection

TREWORLAS in Canada Dock, Surrey Commercial Docks, London, 28th March 1953
following discharge of a cargo of lumber and wheat from
New Westminster
K. Ingram Collection

Estuary. After refloating she was beached off Sheerness where overhanging obstructions were removed. The tow to the River Tyne was restarted and she arrived *1.12.1944,* having put into Leith on account of bad weather. A new fore-part was ordered and launched *5.1946.* After fitting to the original after-part, the vessel was renamed TREWORLAS. *1956:* Transferred to P. and O. Steam Navigation Company. *1958:* Returned to The Hain Steamship Co. Ltd. *1.6.1960:* Grounded on Madira Reef in the Persian Gulf in position 28.49 N, 48.45 E, and *7.6.1960* refloated. Sailed under her own power for Falmouth where drydocked and declared a constructive total loss. Sold to British Iron and Steel Corporation for demolition and sailed from Falmouth *18.9.1960* in tow of the tug TRADESMAN 592/44. *21.9.1960:* Arrived at Briton Ferry where work was commenced by Thomas W. Ward Ltd.

TREVIDER

130. TREVIDER (IV) (1944 — 1955)
O.N. 169843. 7376g, 5133n. 432.6 (447.2 o.l.) × 57.9 × 35.3 feet.
6-cyl. 4 S.C.S.A. Burmeister & Wain oil engine by Harland and Wolff Ltd., Glasgow.
15.2.1944: Launched by Lithgows Ltd., Port Glasgow (Yard No. 986), for The Hain Steamship Co. Ltd. *5.1944:* Completed. *22.8.1955:* Sold to Turnbull Scott Shipping Co. Ltd., (Turnbull, Scott and Co., managers), London, and renamed EASTGATE. *1956:* Sold to Navigation Maritime Bulgare, Bulgaria and renamed BALKAN. *16.1.1968:* Reported aground on rocks off Lattakia, Syria with her engine room and holds flooded while on a voyage from Bourgas to Lattakia with a cargo of grain. *24.7.1968:* Refloated and taken in tow for Bulgaria, but sold to Brodospas, Yugoslavia, for demolition, and arrived *4.8.1968* at Split.

TREVETHOE   *Welsh Industrial & Maritime Museum*

131. TREVETHOE (IV) (1944 — 1951) (1958 — 1959)
O.N. 169895. 7355g, 5004n. 431.0 (444.8 o.l.) × 56.5 × 35.5 feet.
3-cyl. 2 S.C.S.A. oil engine by the Shipbuilder.
18.2.1944: Launched by W. Doxford and Sons Ltd., Sunderland (Yard No. 715), for The Hain Steamship Co. Ltd. *6.1944:* Completed. *1951:* Transferred to P. and O. Steam Navigation Company. *1958:* Returned to The Hain Steamship Co. Ltd. *16.3.1959:* Sold for £143,000 to Herculiania Compania Maritima S.A., Greece, and renamed ALCYONIS. *1969:* Sold to Nan Feng Steel Enterprises Co. Ltd., for demolition and arrived *13.8.1969* at Kaohsiung, Taiwan. *10.1969:* Work commenced.

TREVOSE   *Welsh Industrial & Maritime Museum*

132.   TREVOSE (IV) (1944 — 1951) (1958 — 1962)
O.N. 169931. 7354g, 5006n. 431.0 (444.8 o.l.) × 56.5 × 35.5 feet.
3-cyl. 2 S.C.S.A. oil engine by the Shipbuilder.
25.4.1944: Launched by W. Doxford and Sons Ltd., Sunderland (Yard No. 716), for The Hain
Steamship Co. Ltd. *8.1944:* Completed. *1951:* Transferred to P. and O. Steam Navigation
Company. *1958:* Returned to The Hain Steamship Co. Ltd. *1962:* Sold to Red Anchor Line Ltd.
(Chris. Moller, manager), Hong Kong. (London registry retained) and renamed RUTHY ANN.
9.9.1968: Ran aground following a collision at Haiphong, North Vietnam during a typhoon. She
was refloated *30.9.1968* and was reported to be heavily damaged. Subsequently repaired and
returned to service. *1971:* Sold to Chinese Mainland shipbreakers and sailed from Hong Kong
1.2.1971 bound for Whampoa, where she was delivered *11.2.1971.*

TRESILLIAN leaving London for Japan 25th March 1953 with a full cargo   *T. Rayner*

133.   REGISTAN/TRESILLIAN (IV) (1945 — 1951)
O.N. 180022. 7368g, 5039n. 431.0 (444.8 o.l.) × 56.5 × 35.5 feet.
3-cyl. 2 S.C.S.A. oil engine by the Shipbuilder.
8.1944: Launched by W. Doxford and Sons Ltd., Sunderland (Yard No. 720), as REGISTAN for
Strick Line (1923) Ltd. (F. C. Strick and Co. Ltd., managers), London. *12.1944:* Completed. *1945:*
Purchased by The Hain Steamship Co Ltd. and *1946* renamed TRESILLIAN. *1951:* Transferred
to P. and O. Steam Navigation Company. *30.11.1954:* Capsized and sank when her cargo shifted
in heavy weather 25 miles off Ballycotton, Irish Republic. She was on passage from Montreal to
Avonmouth with a cargo of grain.

TREVEAN   W.S.P.L.

134.   TREVEAN (IV) (1946 — 1957)(1958 — 1963)
O.N. 181116. 7312g, 4748n. 429.0 (442.9 o.l.) × 56.5 × 35.5 feet.
3-cyl. 2 S.C.S.A. oil engine by the Shipbuilder.
9.7.1945: Launched by W. Doxford and Sons Ltd., Sunderland (Yard No. 732), as EMPIRE
TILBURY for The Ministry of War Transport (later Ministry of Transport), W. Runciman and Co.
Ltd., Newcastle, appointed managers. *12.1945:* Completed. *27.3.1946:* Purchased by The Hain
Steamship Co. Ltd., and renamed TREVEAN. *1957:* Transferred to P. and O. Steam Navigation
Company. *1958:* Returned to The Hain Steamship Co. Ltd. *1963:* Sold to Willow Shipping Co.
Ltd. (Eastern Asia Naviation Co. Ltd., managers), Hong Kong, (London registry retained) and
renamed EAST LION. *1964:* Renamed KAWANA. *4.6.1966:* Beached near Chittagong, Pakistan
after fire had broken out in the cargo of coal with which she had arrived *23.5.1966* from
Chinwangtao, China. *20.6.1966:* Reported that her back had broken and declared a total loss.

135.   TRELYON (IV) (1948 — 1963)
O.N. 183048. 5414g, 3049n. 427.6 (442.9 o.l.) × 56.5 × 26.5 feet.
4-cyl. 2 S.C.S.A. oil engine by the Shipbuilder.
17.12.1948: Launched by W. Doxford and Sons Ltd., Sunderland (Yard No. 767), for The Hain
Steamship Co. Ltd. *7.1949:* Completed. *1963:* Sold for £100,000 to Chiao Mao Enterprises Ltd.,
Hong Kong, and renamed YUNGLUTATON. *1967:* Yick Fung Shipping and Enterprises Co. Ltd.
appointed managers. *1974:* Transferred to China Ocean Shipping Company, People's Republic
of China. Later reported transferred to the Government of The People's Republic of China
(Shanghai Port Affairs Administration). Renamed HUA SHAN. Believed still in service.

TRELYON   *St. Ives Museum*

88

TRELAWNY   *K. O'Donoghue Collection*

136. TRELAWNY (IV) (1949 — 1963)
O.N. 183080. 5414g, 3049n. 427.6 (442.9 o.l.) × 56.5 × 26.5 feet.
4-cyl. 2 S.C.S.A. oil engine by the Shipbuilder.
14.1.1949: Launched by W. Doxford and Sons Ltd., Sunderland (Yard No. 768), for The Hain
Steamship Co. Ltd. *8.1949:* Completed. *1963:* Sold for £130,000 to Great Eastern Shipping Co.
Ltd., India, and renamed JAG RAHAT. *1969:* Sold to Sotir Compania Aseguratora y Maritima,
Cyprus and renamed PANAGIA ODIGITRIA. *1972:* Owners restyled Pantocrator Compania
Aseguratora y Maritima S.A. of Panama. *1974:* Sold to Gujranwala Steel Industries Ltd. Pakistan
for demolition and arrived *9.8.1974* at Karachi.

137. TREGENNA (V) (1949 — 1959)
O.N. 183073. 5815g, 3206n. 435.2 (453.3 o.l.) × 57.6 × 25.9 feet.
T.3-cyl. by the shipbuilders, with low pressure turbine, double reduction gearing and hydraulic
coupling.
16.2.1949: Launched by J. Readhead and Sons Ltd., South Shields (Yard No. 564), for The Hain
Steamship Co. Ltd. *8.1949:* Completed. *10.12.1959:* Sold for £205,000 to Pan-Islamic S.S. Co.
Ltd., Pakistan and renamed SAFINA-E-NUSRAT. *1975:* Sold to Pakistan shipbreakers and
demolition commenced *6.1976* at Gadani Beach.

TREGENNA   *Welsh Industrial & Maritime Museum*

TRELISSICK in the Welland Canal   *K. Ingram Collection*

138.   TRELISSICK (III) (1949 — 1963)
O.N. 183107. 5386g, 3055n. 427.6 (442.9 o.l.) × 56.5 × 26.5 feet.
4-cyl. 2 S.C.S.A. oil engine by the Shipbuilder.
2.3.1949: Launched by W. Doxford and Sons Ltd., Sunderland (Yard No. 769), for The Hain
Steamship Co. Ltd. *9.1949:* Completed. *1963:* Sold to Chiao Mao Enterprises Ltd., Hong Kong,
and renamed KINROSS. *1967:* Yick Fung Shipping and Enterprises Co. Ltd., appointed managers.
1972: Registered under Yick Fung Shipping and Enterprises Co., Ltd., Somali Republic. *1974:*
Transferred to China Ocean Shipping Company, People's Republic of China. Believed still in
service.

TRELEVAN

139.   TRELEVAN (II) (1949 — 1964)
O.N. 183132. 5386g, 3055n. 427.6 (442.9 o.l.) × 56.5 × 26.5 feet.
4-cyl. 2 S.C.S.A. oil engine by the Shipbuilder.
15.3.1949 Launched by W. Doxford and Sons Ltd., Sunderland (Yard No. 770), for The Hain Steamship Co. Ltd. *11.1949:* Completed. *1964:* Sold for £165,000 to Cambay Prince S.S. Co. Ltd. (John Manners and Co. Ltd., managers), Hong Kong, and renamed SYDNEY BREEZE. *1970:* Sold to Global Navigation Ltd., Canada, and renamed GLOBAL ENVOY. *1973:* Renamed BAFFIN BAY. *5.7.1973:* Considerably damaged by fire which broke out in the engine room while she was lying at Halifax, Nova Scotia. She had arrived at the port in tow *24.6.1973* after developing engine trouble during a voyage from Montreal to Haiti with a cargo of grain. The fire was extinguished *6.7.1973* and after examination the vessel was sold to Industrial Machinery Corporation, Panama, who then sold her to Marine Salvage, Port Colborne, Ontario. Resold through Jacq. Pierot Junior and Sons to Spanish shipbreakers. *2.1974:* Demolition commenced.

TREGOTHNAN   *Skyfotos*

140.   TREGOTHNAN (II) (1949 — 1959)
O.N. 183141. 5815g, 3206n. 435.2 (453.3 o.l.) × 57.6 × 25.9 feet.
T.3-cyl. by the shipbuilders, with low pressure turbine, double reduction gearing and hydraulic coupling.
12.7.1949: Launched by J. Readhead and Sons Ltd., South Shields (Yard No. 565), for The Hain Steamship Co. Ltd. *11.1949:* Completed. *1959:* Sold for £207,500 to Trans Oceanic S.S. Co. Ltd., Pakistan, and renamed OCEAN ENTERPRISE. *9.12.1971:* Heavily damaged in an Indian air attack when berthed at Chalna, Pakistan. No subsequent reports, but assumed broken up.

91

TREGLISSON

141. TREGLISSON (III) (1949 — 1960)
O.N. 183212. 5270g, 3281n. 435.5 (453.0 o.l.) × 57.5 × 26.0 feet.
T.3-cyl. by D. Rowan and Co. Ltd., Glasgow, with low pressure turbine double reduction gearing and hydraulic coupling.
20.10.1949: Launched by Wm. Hamilton and Co. Ltd., Port Glasgow (Yard No. 484), for The Hain Steamship Co. Ltd. *3.1950:* Completed. *29.3.1960:* Sold for £215,000 to United Oriental S.S. Company, Pakistan, and renamed YOUSUFBAKSH. *8.5.1965:* Beached near Deal after a fire had broken out in her cargo of jute while on a voyage from Chittagong, Pakistan to Boulogne. She was refloated *28.5.1965* but grounded again the following day. *31.5.1965:* Again refloated and *1.6.1965* arrived in tow at Rotterdam where her cargo was discharged. Found to be beyond economical repair and sold to German shipbreakers. *23.1.1966:* Demolition commenced at Hamburg by Eisen & Metall A.G.

TRELOSKE

142. TRELOSKE (IV) (1949 — 1963)
O.N. 183219. 5386g, 3055n. 427.6 (442.9 o.l.) × 56.5 × 26.5 feet.
4-cyl. 2 S.C.S.A. oil engine by the Shipbuilder.
9.8.1949: Launched by W. Doxford and Sons Ltd., Sunderland (Yard No. 774), for The Hain Steamship Co. Ltd. *4.1950:* Completed. *1963:* Sold for £100,000 to Chiao Mao Enterprises Ltd., Hong Kong, and renamed YUNGFUTARY. *26.7.1968:* Ran aground some 300 miles N.E. of Hong Kong on rocks off Fukien Province, S.E. China, and was declared a total loss. She was on a voyage from Shanghai to Singapore with general cargo.

TREMAYNE   *F. R. Sherlock*

143. TREMAYNE (III) (1952 — 1968)
O.N. 185848. 5608g, 3131n. 436.5 (455.5 o.l.) × 58.2 × 26.0 feet.
4-cyl. 2 S.C.S.A. Doxford oil engine by D. Rowan and Co. Ltd., Glasgow.
17.9.1952: Launched by Wm. Hamilton and Co. Ltd., Port Glasgow (Yard No. 493), for The Hain
Steamship Co. Ltd. *3.1953:* Completed. *1.10.1965:* Registered under Hain-Nourse Ltd. *1968:*
Sold to Vasa Shipping Co. Ltd., Cyprus, and renamed VIRGY. *1973:* A. Halcoussis & Co. appointed
managers. *1975:* Sold to Fury Shipping Company Ltd., Cyprus, and renamed ILION. *1979:* Sold
to M/S Yashma Ltd., Pakistan, but not delivered due to litigation. Arrived and anchored *22.5.1979*
off Karachi. *7.8.1979:* Ran aground close to the Manora Lighthouse, but no attempt was made
to refloat her. Sold to local shipbreakers and demolition commenced "in situ" during *12.1979.*

TREMORVAH   *Welsh Industrial & Maritime Museum*

144. TREMORVAH (III) (1954 — 1968)
O.N. 186088. 5605g, 3032n. 436.5 (455.5 o.l.) × 58.2 × 26.0 feet.
4-cyl. 2 S.C.S.A. Doxford oil engine by D. Rowan and Co. Ltd., Glasgow.
7.5.1954: Launched by Wm. Hamilton and Co. Ltd., Port Glasgow (Yard No. 494), for The Hain
Steamship Co. Ltd. *7.1954:* Completed. *1.10.1965:* Registered under Hain-Nourse Ltd.
18.1.1968: Sold to Sancherouvim Compania Maritima S.A., Greece, and renamed ARCHON
CHERUBIM. *1974:* Sold to Caledon Bay Shipping Company, Panama, and renamed FIVE HILLS.
1976: Sold to Victoria Navigation Co. Ltd., Panama, and renamed PHUTRUKSA. *1978:* Sold to
Sam Woo, Hong Kong, for demolition. *14.9.1978:* Work commenced.

TREMEADOW   V. H. Young

145. TREMEADOW (III) (1957 — 1972)
O.N. 187723. 6504g, 3415n. 471' 9" × 61' 3" × 26' 6½".
4-cyl. 2 S.C.S.A. Doxford oil engine by D. Rowan and Co. Ltd., Glasgow.
7.11.1957: Launched by Wm. Hamilton and Co. Ltd., Port Glasgow (Yard No. 514), for The Hain
Steamship Co. Ltd. *1.1958:* Completed. *1.10.1965:* Registered under Hain-Nourse Ltd.
1.10.1971: P. and O. General Cargo Division appointed managers. *1972:* Registered under
Peninsular and Oriental Steam Navigation Company. *11.12.1973:* Sold to Gulf Shipping Lines
Ltd. (Wallem Shipmanagement Ltd., managers), London, and renamed RELIANCE EXPRESS.
1975: Gulfeast Ship Management Ltd. appointed managers. *1976:* Renamed GULF RELIANCE.
1980: Sold to Nan Long Steel and Iron Co. Ltd., Taiwan and demolition commenced *2.5.1980* at
Kaohsiung.

TRECARRELL

146. TRECARRELL (III) (1959 — 1971)
O.N. 300862. 6499g, 3388n. 471' 9" × 61' 3" × 26' 6½".
4-cyl. 2 S.C.S.A. Doxford oil engine by D. Rowan and Co. Ltd., Glasgow.
8.1.1959: Launched by Wm. Hamilton and Co. Ltd., Port Glasgow (Yard No. 518), for The Hain
Steamship Co. Ltd. *3.1959:* Completed. *1.10.1965:* Registered under Hain-Nourse Ltd. *1971:*
Sold to Seven Isles Shipping Corporation, Cyprus, and renamed SKIPPER. *1972:* Sold to Saint
John Shipping Co. Ltd., Cyprus. *1974:* Sold to Elefinor Shipping Company S.A., Cyprus, and *1975*
renamed DELPHI. *1976:* Resold to Saint John Shipping Co. Ltd., Cyprus. *1977:* Sold to Green
River Inc. (Belgravia Maritime Corp., managers), Greece, and renamed ALTONA. *4.5.1979:*
Abandoned by her crew when a boiler explosion resulted in a severe fire while passing through
the Straits of Gibraltar, on a voyage from Dunkirk to Kuwait. Beached *5.5.1979* near the entrance
to Puerto de Santa Maria, Cadiz, in position 30.05 N, 06.26 W. She was refloated and following
examination sold to Maslia S.A. for demolition. *27.8.1979:* Arrived Cartagena in tow from Cadiz
and *1.1980* demolition commenced.

TREVAYLOR at Cape Town in 1970   *V. H. Young*

147. TREVAYLOR (IV) (1959 — 1972)
O.N. 300882. 6501g, 3388n. 471' 9" × 61' 3" × 26' 6½".
4-cyl. 2 S.C.S.A. Doxford oil engine by the Shipbuilder.
23.1.1959: Launched by Barclay, Curle and Co. Ltd., Glasgow (Yard No. 741), for The Hain Steamship Co. Ltd. *4.1959:* Completed. *1.10.1965:* Registered under Hain-Nourse Ltd. *1.10.1971:* P. and O. General Cargo Division appointed managers. *1972:* Registered under Peninsular and Oriental Steam Navigation Company. *26.1.1973:* Sold to Gerontina Compania Naviera S.A. Panama, Greece, and renamed EVGENIA I. *11.2.1976:* Grounded 23 miles N. of Jeddah when on passage from Houston to Hodeidah, Yemen with general cargo. She was quickly refloated but was promptly beached due to severe bottom damage. Much of her cargo was subsequently discharged but attempts to refloat her were unsuccessful and she was abandoned as a total loss.

TRECARNE

148. TRECARNE (II) (1959 — 1972)
O.N. 300974. 6499g, 3381n. 471' 9" × 61' 3" × 26' 6¼".
4-cyl. 2 S.C.S.A. Doxford oil engine by D. Rowan and Co. Ltd., Glasgow.
6.5.1959: Launched by Wm. Hamilton and Co. Ltd., Port Glasgow (Yard No. 519), for The Hain Steamship Co. Ltd. *8.1959:* Completed. *1.10.1965:* Registered under Hain-Nourse Ltd. *1.10.1971:* P. and O. General Cargo Division appointed managers. *1972:* Registered under Peninsular and Oriental Steam Navigation Company. *20.3.1974:* Sold to Golden Arrow Shipping Co. Ltd., Cyprus, and renamed GOLDEN ARROW. *1976:* Sold to East Arrow Compania Naviera S.A., Greece. *25.10.1976:* Arrived at Hodeidah, with her engine room flooded, during a voyage from Damman, and was subsequently laid up. Considered to be beyond economical repair, and sold to Premier Shipbreaking Company, Pakistan. Sailed from Hodeidah *3.10.1978* bound in tow for Karachi, anchoring off the port *28.10.1978.* Later moved on to Gadani Beach for demolition, arriving prior to 7.12.1978.

TREWIDDEN   *W.S.S.-Brownell Collection*

149. TREWIDDEN (V) (1960 — 1972)
O.N. 301146. 6671g, 3352n. 488' 0" × 63' 3" × 26' 5¾".
4-cyl. 2 S.C.S.A. Doxford oil engine by Wallsend Slipway and Engineering Co. Ltd., Wallsend.
26.2.1960: Launched by J. Readhead and Sons Ltd., South Shields (Yard No. 604), for The Hain
Steamship Co. Ltd. *6.1960:* Completed. *1.10.1965:* Registered under Hain-Nourse Ltd.
1.10.1971: P. and O. General Cargo Division appointed managers. *1972:* Registered under
Peninsular and Oriental Steam Navigation Company. *18.6.1975:* Sold to Epiktetos Shipping Co.
Ltd., Cyprus, and renamed SARINA I. *6.6.1978:* Reported disabled off Somalia in a position
08.31 N, 50.43 E, with main engine damage. She was on a voyage from Aqaba to Tanzania with
a cargo of bulk phosphate. Taken in tow, and *26.6.1978* arrived at Tanga, where she was
discharged. Subsequently offered for sale by order of the District Registrar of Tanga and purchased
for demolition by Aluminium Africa Ltd. Resold through West German interests to Nan Long Steel
and Iron Co. Ltd., Taiwan, and arrived *11.12.1979* at Kaohsiung. *26.12.1979:* Demolition
commenced.

150. TREVALGAN (IV) (1960 — 1972)
O.N. 302610. 6706g, 3407n. 487' 11" × 63' 3" × 26' 5½".
6-cyl. 2 S.C.S.A. Sulzer oil engine by D. Rowan and Co. Ltd., Glasgow.
6.12.1960: Launched by Wm. Hamilton and Co. Ltd., Port Glasgow (Yard No. 523), for The Hain
Steamship Co. Ltd. *3.1961:* Completed. *1.10.1965:* Registered under Hain-Nourse Ltd.
1.10.1971: P. and O. General Cargo Division appointed managers. *1972:* Registered under
Peninsular and Oriental Steam Navigation Company. *5.1.1973:* Sold to Evalend Shipping
Company S.A., Greece, and renamed LENDOUDIS EVANGELOS. *1982:* Registered at Panama.
1985: Sold to Eastern Ship Breakers, Bangladesh, and *4.2.1985* arrived at Chittagong. *7.3.1985:*
Demolition commenced at Bhatiary.

TREVALGAN   *J. Clarkson*

TREFUSIS *Airfoto, Malacca*

151. TREFUSIS (III) (1961 — 1972)
O.N. 302856. 10077g, 5754n. 508' 3" × 65' 3" × 29' 0¼".
5-cyl. 2 S.C.S.A. Sulzer oil engine by Wallsend Slipway and Engineering Co. Ltd., Wallsend.
11.9.1961: Launched by J. Readhead and Sons Ltd., South Shields (Yard No. 609), for The Hain Steamship Co. Ltd. *12.1961:* Completed. *1.10.1965:* Registered under Hain-Nourse Ltd. *1.10.1971:* P. and O. General Cargo Division appointed managers. *1972:* Registered under Peninsular and Oriental Steam Navigation Company. *11.7.1975:* Renamed STRATHTEVIOT. *19.1.1978:* Sold to Kodros Shipping Corporation (Olistim Navigation Company, managers), Greece, and renamed EVIA. *23.9.1980:* Detained at Basrah as a result of the Iran-Iraq hostilities. Still in port.

152. TREBARTHA (II) (1962 — 1972)
O.N. 302985. 10148g, 5754n. 508' 3" × 65' 3" × 29' 9".
5-cyl. 2 S.C.S.A. Sulzer oil engine by Wallsend Slipway and Engineering Co. Ltd., Wallsend.
23.1.1962: Launched by J. Readhead and Sons Ltd., South Shields (Yard No. 610), for The Hain Steamship Co. Ltd. *5.1962:* Completed. *1.10.1965:* Registered under Hain-Nourse Ltd. *1.10.1971:* P. and O. General Cargo Division appointed managers. *1972:* Registered under Peninsular and Oriental Steam Navigation Company. *7.5.1975:* Renamed STRATHTAY. *25.1.1978:* Sold to Marikog Shipping Company S.A., Panama, and renamed ZAK. *1985:* Sold to Chinese shipbreakers and *9.1.1985* arrived at Lianyungang.

TREBARTHA at Rotterdam July 1969 *V. H. Young*

97

TRENEGLOS

153. TRENEGLOS (V) (1963)
O.N. 304673. 9976g, 5793n. 505' 3" × 65' 3" × 27' 1½".
5-cyl. 2 S.C.S.A. Sulzer oil engine by Fairfield-Rowan Ltd., Glasgow.
28.3.1963: Launched by Wm. Hamilton and Co. Ltd., Port Glasgow (Yard No. 527), as TRENEGLOS for The Hain Steamship Co. Ltd. but completed *8.1963* for New Zealand Shipping Co. Ltd., London. *12.11.1964:* Grounded 1¼ miles S. of Timaru whilst on a voyage from Timaru to Dunedin. Refloated *17.11.1964* with considerable damage. *30.9.1968:* Registered under Hain-Nourse Ltd. *1.10.1971:* P. and O. General Cargo Division appointed managers. *1972:* Registered under Peninsular and Oriental Steam Navigation Company. *28.11.1974:* Renamed STRATHTRUIM. *27.1.1978:* Sold to Torenia Maritime Inc. (Zodiac Maritime Agencies Ltd., managers), Singapore, and renamed SIAM BAY. *1979:* Sold to Chrysalis Compania Naviera S.A. (Family Shipping Co. S.A. Panama, managers), Greece, and renamed FAMILY ANGEL. *1984:* Sold to Temple S.A., Panama, and renamed DOMAN. *1985:* Sold to Chinese shipbreakers and arrived *2.8.1985* at Nantong.

HAIN-NOURSE LTD.

BETWA

HN1. BETWA (1965 — 1966)
O.N. 183296. 6722g, 4009n. 431'10" × 55'.3" × 27'6¼".
3-cyl. 2 S.C.S.A. Doxford oil engine by Barclay, Curle and Co. Ltd., Glasgow.
2.6.1950: Launched by C. Connell and Co. Ltd., Glasgow (Yard No. 465), as BETWA for James Nourse Ltd., London. *8.1950:* Completed. *1.10.1965:* Registered under Hain-Nourse Ltd. *1966:* Sold to British India Steam Navigation Co. Ltd., London and renamed SIRSA. *1.10.1971:* P. and O. General Cargo Division appointed managers. *1971:* Sold to Ming Hing and Co. Ltd., Hong Kong, for demolition and *18.11.1971* delivered.

INDUS

HN2. INDUS (1965 — 1969)
O.N. 186125. 7049g, 4036n. 440'6" × 58'2" × 27'7".
4-cyl. 2 S.C.S.A. Doxford oil engine by Barclay, Curle and Co. Ltd., Glasgow.
5.7.1954: Launched by C. Connell and Co. Ltd., Glasgow (Yard No. 475), as INDUS for James Nourse Ltd., London. *9.1954:* Completed. *1.10.1965:* Registered under Hain-Nourse Ltd. *13.11.1969:* Sold to Societa Armadora Insular S.A., Liberia and renamed SPILIADA. *1970:* Sold to Naves Transatlantica S.A. & Ktimatikai Epichirisis Athinon A.E., Greece. *1974:* Sold to Ahli Shipping Lines (Great Circle Line Inc., managers), Dubai, and renamed AHLI. *1979:* Sold to Caravaneau Navigation Ltd., S.A., Panama, and renamed SEA PROSPERITY. *1979:* Sold to Silver Line Trading Corp., Panana, and renamed GULF MOON. *1980:* Sold to Karim Shipbreaking Industries Ltd., Pakistan for demolition, and arrived *28.6.1980* at Gadani Beach. *5.9.1980:* Demolition commenced.

ERNE

HN3. ERNE (1965 — 1969)   (Tanker)
O.N. 302981. 14244g, 8241n. 559'9" × 71'11" × 31'0¾".
Two steam turbines by Barclay, Curle and Co. Ltd., Glasgow, double reduction geared to single screw shaft.
11.11.1961: Launched by C. Connell and Co. Ltd., Glasgow (Yard No. 493), as ERNE for James Nourse Ltd., London. *2.1962:* Completed. *10.5.1963:* Trident Tankers Ltd. appointed managers. *1.10.1965:* Registered under Hain-Nourse Ltd. *1.4.1969:* Transferred to Trident Tankers Ltd. *16.8.1971:* Management taken over by P. and O. Bulk Shipping Division. *27.9.1972:* Registered under Peninsular and Oriental Steam Navigation Company. *1984:* Sold to Sing Cheng Yung Iron and Steel Co. Ltd., Taiwan and demolition commenced *14.7.1984* at Kaohsiung.

JUMNA   *V. H. Young*

HN4.   JUMNA (1965 — 1972)
O.N. 304391. 10051g, 5792n. 508'3" × 65'3" × 30'9".
5-cyl. 2 S.C.S.A. Sulzer oil engine by Barclay, Curle and Co. Ltd., Glasgow.
28.9.1962: Launched by C. Connell and Co. Ltd., Glasgow (Yard No. 495), as JUMNA for James Nourse Ltd., London. *11.1962:* Completed. *1.10.1965:* Registered under Hain-Nourse Ltd. *1.10.1971:* P. and O. General Cargo Division appointed managers. *11.5.1972:* Registered under Peninsular and Oriental Steam Navigation Company. *1975:* Renamed STRATHNAVER. *1977:* Sold to Proteas Maritime Inc., Singapore, and renamed SINGAPORE PROGRESS. *1979:* Renamed DELTA. *1980:* Sold to Alfa Maritime Company S.A. (Antonios Catsogeorgis, manager), Greece, and renamed FAMILY DELTA. *1985:* Sold to Indian shipbreakers.

100

KOHINUR on charter to Hamburg-Sudamerikanische D/S at Rotterdam
in June 1971   *V. H. Young*

HN5.   KOHINUR (1968 — 1972)
O.N. 304468. 10039g, 5851n. 508'3" × 65'3" × 30'1¼".
5-cyl. 2 S.C.S.A. Sulzer oil engine by Barclay, Curle and Co. Ltd., Glasgow.
28.12.1962: Launched by C. Connell and Co. Ltd., Glasgow (Yard No. 500), as KOHINUR for New
Zealand Shipping Co. Ltd., London. (She had been ordered for Asiatic Steam Navigation Co. Ltd.,
London). *3.1963:* Completed. *1.10.1965:* Hain-Nourse Ltd. appointed managers. *30.9.1968:*
Registered under Hain-Nourse Ltd. *1.10.1971:* P. and O. General Cargo Division appointed
managers. *11.5.1972:* Registered under Peninsular and Oriental Steam Navigation Company.
1975: Renamed STRATHNAIRN. *1977:* Sold to British Bay Shipping Co. Ltd., Singapore and
renamed SILVERGATE. *1979:* Renamed ANTILLA. *1986:* Sold to Taiwan shipbreakers and arrived
21.3.1986 at Kaohsiung.

ADVOCATE on charter to T. & J. Harrison Ltd.   *W.S.P.L.*

HN6.   NURJEHAN/ADVOCATE (1968 — 1972)
O.N. 304514. 8380g, 4731n. 481'9" × 62'6" × 29'8".
5-cyl. 2 S.C.S.A. Burmeister & Wain oil engine by J. G. Kincaid and Co. Ltd., Greenock.
29.1.1963: Launched by Lithgows Ltd., Port Glasgow (Yard No. 1122), as NURJEHAN for New
Zealand Shipping Co. Ltd., London. (She had been ordered for Asiatic Steam Navigation Co. Ltd.,
London). *4.1963:* Completed. *1.10.1965:* Hain-Nourse Ltd. appointed managers. *30.9.1968:*
Registered under Hain-Nourse Ltd. *1971:* Chartered to Charente S.S. Co. Ltd. (T. and J. Harrison
Ltd., managers), Liverpool and renamed ADVOCATE. *1.10.1971:* P. and O. General Cargo Division
appointed managers. *1972:* Registered under Peninsular and Oriental Steam Navigation
Company. *1973:* Renamed NURJEHAN upon expiration of the charter. *1975:* Renamed
STRATHNEVIS. *1977:* Sold to Unimed Shipping Inc., Greece, and renamed IOANNIS. *1982:* Sold
to Dafnopotamos Maritime Corp. (Loutra Shipping and General Enterprises Ltd., managers),
Greece, and renamed DIMITRIOS P. PAPASTRATIS. *1984:* Sold to Indian shipbreakers and arrived
at an Indian port prior to *13.10.1984.*

VESSELS MANAGED ON BEHALF OF
MERCANTILE STEAM SHIP CO. LTD.

A1. AYR (1917 — 1918)
O.N. 104796. 3050g, 1955n. 322.0 × 41.6 × 21.5 feet.
T.3-cyl. by J. Dickinson and Sons Ltd., Sunderland.
6.6.1894: Launched by J. L. Thompson and Sons Ltd., Sunderland (Yard No. 318), for Mercantile Steam Ship Co. Ltd., London. *9.1894:* Completed. *1917:* E. Hain and Son appointed managers.
8.3.1918: Torpedoed and sunk 31 miles N¼W from Linosa Island, Sicily, by a German submarine.

NESS   *E. N. Taylor*

A2. NESS (1917)
O.N. 105788. 3050g, 1963n. 322.0 × 41.5 × 21.4 feet.
T.3-cyl. by J. Dickinson and Sons Ltd., Sunderland.
17.12.1895: Launched by J. L. Thompson and Sons Ltd., Sunderland (Yard No. 339), for Mercantile Steam Ship Co. Ltd., London. *1.1896:* Completed. *1917:* E. Hain and Son appointed managers. *25.10.1917:* Captured by the German submarine U.64, 10 miles S.E. from Cabo de Gata, Spain and sunk by gunfire.

A3. MIN (I) (1917 — 1920)
O.N. 108262. 3083g, 1981n. 325.0 × 44.5 × 19.7 feet.
T.3-cyl. by T. Richardson and Sons Ltd., Hartlepool.
12.8.1897: Launched by J. L. Thompson and Sons Ltd., Sunderland (Yard No. 353), for Mercantile Steam Ship Co. Ltd., London. *11.1897:* Completed. *1917:* E. Hain and Son appointed managers. *1920:* Sold to Destouni Frères, Greece and renamed VASSILIOS DESTOUNIS. *1928:* Registered under B. Destounis Frères (Ath. Xanthopoulo Sons & Co., managers), Greece. *1932:* Sold to Italian shipbreakers at Savona.

A4. DART (1917)
O.N. 108395. 3207g, 2056n. 325.0 × 44.5 × 19.7 feet.
T.3-cyl. by T. Richardson and Sons Ltd., Hartlepool.
25.5.1898: Launched by J. L. Thompson and Sons Ltd., Sunderland (Yard No. 363), for Mercantile Steam Ship Co. Ltd., London. *7.1898:* Completed. *1917:* E. Hain and Son appointed managers.
14.6.1917: Torpedoed and sunk 6 miles S.S.W. from Ballycotton Lighthouse.

GANGES   *E. N. Taylor*

A5. GANGES (1917)
O.N. 114821. 4177g, 2721n. 360.2 x 46.9 x 17.9 feet.
T.3-cyl. by J. Dickinson and Sons Ltd., Sunderland.
26.11.1901: Launched by Bartram and Sons, Sunderland (Yard No. 185), for Mercantile Steam Ship Co. Ltd., London. *1.1902:* Completed. *1917:* E. Hain and Son appointed managers.
30.7.1917: Torpedoed and sunk 8 miles S.W. from Cape Spartel, Morocco.

LENA   *E. N. Taylor*

A6. LENA (1917 — 1923)
O.N. 115850. 4146g, 2679n. 345.0 x 48.6 x 25.9 feet.
T.3-cyl. by Richardsons, Westgarth and Co. Ltd., Hartlepool.
24.4.1902: Launched by J. L. Thompson and Sons Ltd., Sunderland (Yard No. 399), for Mercantile Steam Ship Co. Ltd., London. *7.1902:* Completed. *1917:* E. Hain and Son appointed managers.
1923: Sold to N. G. Lyras, Greece and renamed MARIGO L. *1934:* Sold to Italian shipbreakers and broken up at La Spezia.

A7. BOYNE (1917 — 1923)
See BOYNE (No 103).

A8. FOYLE (1917 — 1923)
See FOYLE (No. 104).

A9. PRUTH (1917 — 1923)
See PRUTH (No. 105).

A10. MIN (II) (1922 — 1923)
See MIN (No. 102).

MIN

VESSELS MANAGED BY THE HAIN STEAMSHIP CO. LTD.
AND ITS SUCCESSORS FOR P&O STEAM NAVIGATION CO.
AND ITS SUBSIDIARIES

This list does not include Hain vessels that were transferred to P&O ownership for short periods, which are included in the main fleet list.

B1. JEYPORE (1928 — 1934) (1941 — 1942)
O.N. 137273. 5318g, 3209n. 400.0 × 52.3 × 28.4 feet.
T. 3-cyl. by Central Marine Engine Works, West Hartlepool.
5.2.1920: Launched by Wm. Gray and Co. (1918) Ltd., Sunderland (Yard No. 934), as WAR MOTH for The Shipping Controller, London. Purchased and *5.1920* completed as JEYPORE for P&O Steam Navigation Co. *1928:* Management allocated to The Hain Steamship Co. Ltd. *1934:* Management ceased. *26.5.1941:* Management again allocated to Hain. *3.11.1942:* Torpedoed and sunk by the German submarine U.89 in the N. Atlantic, S.E. of Cape Farewell, in position 55.30 N, 40.16 W.

B2. LAHORE (1928 — 1934)
O.N. 137272. 5252g, 3143n. 400.6 × 52.3 × 28.5 feet.
T. 3-cyl. by North Eastern Marine Engineering Co. Ltd., Sunderland.
5.2.1920: Launched by R. Thompson and Sons Ltd., Sunderland (Yard No. 312), for P&O Steam Navigation Co. (She had been laid down for The Shipping Controller) *4.1920:* Completed. *1928:* The Hain Steamship Co. Ltd. appointed managers. *8.3.1941:* Torpedoed by the German submarine U.124, N.E. of the Cape Verde Islands in position 21.03 N, 20.38 W. She was abandoned by her crew the following day with her forepart burned out and is presumed to have sunk shortly afterwards. She was on a voyage from Calcutta to London.

B3. NAGPORE (1928 — 1934)
O.N. 144054. 5283g, 3226n. 400.4 × 52.2 × 28.5 feet.
T. 3-cyl. by Richardsons, Westgarth and Co. Ltd., Middlesbrough.
6.6.1920: Launched by Earle's Co. Ltd., Hull (Yard No. 639), for P&O Steam Navigation Co. (She had been laid down for The Shipping Controller). *9.1920:* Completed. *1928:* The Hain Steamship Co. Ltd. appointed managers. *1934:* Management ceased. *28.10.1942:* Torpedoed by the German submarine U.509 and then sunk by torpedo and gunfire from U.203 off the Canary Islands in position 31.30 N, 19.36 W. She was on a voyage from Durban to Manchester.

PADUA   *K. O'Donoghue Collection*

B4. PADUA (1928 — 1933)
O.N. 144312. 5907g, 3678n. 450.8 × 57.2 × 26.9 feet.
T. 3-cyl. by the Shipbuilder.
12.11.1912: Launched by J. C. Tecklenborg A.G., Geestemunde (Yard No. 251), as LUNEBURG for Deutsche-Australische Dampfschiffs-Gesellschaft, Germany. *12.1912:* Completed. *24.8.1919:* Surrendered to Great Britain as a prize and managed for The Shipping Controller by British India Steam Navigation Co. Ltd., London. *3.11.1920:* Purchased by P&O Steam Navigation Co. and renamed PADUA. *1928:* The Hain Steamship Co. Ltd. appointed managers. *3.1933:* Sold for £10,500 to Goshi Kaisha Fukushima Denkichi Shoten for demolition and delivered *29.5.1933* at Osaka.

B5. PERIM (1928 — 1934)
O.N. 143098. 7648g, 4779n. 469.5 × 58.5 × 32.2 feet.
T 3-cyl. by the Shipbuilder.
1916: Launched by J. C. Tecklenborg A.G., Geestemunde (Yard No. 270), as TREUENFELS for Deutsche Dampfschiffs-Gesellschaft "Hansa", Germany. *1919:* Surrendered to Great Britain as a prize and managed for The Shipping Controller by Walter Runciman and Co. Ltd., Newcastle upon Tyne. *22.10.1920:* Purchased by P&O Steam Navigation Co. and renamed PERIM. *1928:* The Hain Steamship Co. Ltd. appointed managers. *1934:* Management ceased. *26.2.1935:* Sold for £11,500 to Metal Industries Ltd. for demolition and delivered *5.3.1935* at Rosyth.

B6. SOMALI (1930 — 1941)
See No. 114 in main fleet.

B7. SOUDAN (1930 — 1942)
O.N. 161939. 6677g, 3477n. 459.0 × 60.7 × 29.8 feet.
Q. 4-cyl. by the Shipbuilder, with low pressure steam turbine.
24.1.1930: Launched by Barclay, Curle and Co. Ltd., Glasgow (Yard No. 643), for P&O Steam Navigation Co. The Hain Steamship Co. Ltd. appointed managers. (Vessel ordered *12.1929* by Hain but sold prior to commencement of construction). *1.1931:* Completed. *15.5.1942:* Mined and sunk off Cape Agulhas, South Africa, whilst on a voyage from Glasgow and Freetown to Durban with military stores. Her crew was rescued.

B8. SHILLONG (1938 — 1943)
O.N. 167175. 5529g, 3253n. 442.2 × 57.9 × 25.7 feet.
4-cyl. 2 S.C.S.A. Doxford oil engine by Barclay, Curle and Co. Ltd., Glasgow.
11.8.1938: Launched by Alexander Stephen and Sons Ltd., Glasgow (Yard No. 562), for P&O Steam Navigation Co. The Hain Steamship Co. Ltd. appointed managers. *2.1939:* Completed. *4.4.1943:* Torpedoed by the German submarine U.635 in the N. Atlantic off Cape Farewell in position 57.10 N, 35.30 W and sank the following day. She was on a voyage from Port Lincoln and New York for Belfast and Swansea with a cargo of zinc concentrates.

B9. SURAT (1938 — 1941)
O.N. 166621. 5529g, 3253n. 442.2 × 57.9 × 25.7 feet.
4-cyl. 2 S.C.S.A. Doxford oil engine by the Shipbuilders.
15.6.1938: Launched by Alexander Stephen and Sons Ltd., Glasgow (Yard No. 561), for P&O Steam Navigation Co. The Hain Steamship Co. Ltd. appointed managers. *1.1939:* Completed. *6.5.1941:* Torpedoed and sunk by the German submarine U.103, W. of Freetown in position 08.23 N, 15.13 W whilst on a voyage from Karachi to the U.K. with a cargo of pig iron and rape seed.

B10. SOCOTRA (1943 — 1946)
O.N. 168430. 7840g, 3864n. 465.7 × 62.9 × 38.3 feet.
Two 4-cyl. 2 S.C.S.A. Doxford oil engines by the Shipbuilders, driving twin screws.
18.3.1943: Launched by Barclay, Curle and Co. Ltd., Glasgow (Yard No. 691), for P&O Steam Navigation Co. The Hain Steamship Co. Ltd. appointed managers. *5.1943:* Completed. *2.8.1946:* Management ceased. *18.6.1965:* Sold to Hong Kong Chiap Hua Mfg. Co. (1947) Ltd. for demolition and *1.7.1965* work commenced.

B11. ATHERSTONE (1965 — 1971) Bulk Carrier
O.N. 306345. 26334g, 18248n. 675' 11" × 90' 2" × 54' 7".
7-cyl. 2 S.C.S.A. Burmeister & Wain oil engine by Hitachi Zosen, Osaka.
9.1.1965: Launched by Hitachi Zosen, Innoshima (Yard No. 4048), for P&O Steam Navigation Co. Hain-Nourse Ltd. appointed managers. *4.1965:* Completed. *1971:* Management transferred to P&O Bulk Shipping Division. *9.5.1978:* Sold to Golden Ocean Development Inc., Liberia, and renamed GOLDEN ALLIANCE. *1982:* Sold to China Ocean Shipping Company, People's Republic of China and renamed YANG MING SHAN. Still in service.

B12. BUCCLEUCH (1965 — 1971) Bulk Carrier
O.N. 307922. 25293g, 16249n. 675' 0" (Inc. B.B.) × 90' 0" × 53' 7½".
7-cyl. 2 S.C.S.A. Burmeister & Wain oil engine by Harland and Wolff Ltd., Belfast.
29.4.1965: Launched by Furness Shipbuilding Co. Ltd., Haverton Hill-on-Tees (Yard No. 521), for British India Steam Navigation Co. Ltd. Hain-Nourse Ltd. appointed managers. *10.1965:* Completed. *1971:* Management transferred to P&O Bulk Shipping Division. *1972:* Registered under P&O Steam Navigation Co. *14.11.1973:* Sold to Knossos Shipping Inc., Liberia, and renamed ARGO CASTOR. *1977:* Renamed ATLANTICO. *1982:* Sold to Vera Shipping Corporation, Liberia, and renamed VERA. *11.8.1983:* Laid up at Piraeus and still there 6.1986.

B13 KOHINUR (1965-1972)
See No. HN5

B14. NURJEHAN/ADVOCATE (1965-1972)
See No. HN6

DUHALLOW   *F. R. Sherlock*

B15. DUHALLOW (1965 — 1971) Bulk Carrier
O.N. 308051. 25368g, 16219n. 675' 0" (Inc. B.B.) × 90' 0" × 53' 6".
7-cyl. 2 S.C.S.A. Burmeister & Wain oil engine by J. G. Kincaid and Co. Ltd., Greenock.
26.10.1965: Launched by Fairfield Shipbuilding and Engineering Co. Ltd., Glasgow (Yard No.
828), for Charter Shipping Co. Ltd. Hain-Nourse Ltd. appointed managers. *3.1966:* Completed.
1971: Management transferred to P&O Bulk Shipping Division. *12.8.1974:* Sold to Mogul Line
Ltd., India, and renamed JANA VIJAY. *1985:* Sold to Rajesh Iron and Steel Works, India, for
demolition and arrived at Port Alang prior to *20.2.1985.*

B16. COTSWOLD (1966 — 1971) Bulk Carrier
O.N. 308133. 25291g, 16304n. 675' 0" (Inc. B.B.) × 90' 0" × 53' 8".
7-cyl. 2 S.C.S.A. Burmeister & Wain oil engine by Harland and Wolff Ltd., Belfast.
7.2.1966: Launched by Furness Shipbuilding Co. Ltd., Haverton Hill-on-Tees (Yard No. 522), for
British India Steam Navigation Co. Ltd. Hain-Nourse Ltd. appointed managers. *5.1966:*
Completed. *1971:* Management transferred to P&O Bulk Shipping Division. *1972:* Registered
under P&O Steam Navigation Co. *12.11.1973:* Sold to Thessaly Shipping Inc., Liberia, and
renamed ARGO POLLUX. *1977:* Renamed PACIFICO. *1982:* Sold to Kalavria Compania Naviera
S.A., Greece, and renamed KALAVRIA. *1986:* Sold to Chinese shipbreakers.

B17. FERNIE (1967 — 1971) Bulk Carrier
O.N. 309922. 42446g, 28857n. 825' 1" (Inc. B.B.) × 105' 8" × 61' 0".
9-cyl. 2 S.C.S.A. Burmeister & Wain oil engine by the Shipbuilder.
9.1.1967: Launched by Mitsui Zosen, Tamano (Yard No. 769), for P&O Steam Navigation Co.
Hain-Nourse Ltd. appointed managers. *6.1967:* Completed. *1971:* Management transferred to
P&O Bulk Shipping Division. *15.1.1979:* Sold to Alcyone Shipping Co., Liberia, and renamed
ALCYONE. *1980:* Sold to Canadian Pacific (Bermuda) Ltd., Hong Kong, and renamed FORT
FRASER. *1985:* Sold to Taiwan shipbreakers and arrived *17.1.1985* at Kaohsiung.

FERNIE   *T. Rayner*

VESSELS MANAGED ON BEHALF OF
THE SHIPPING CONTROLLER

MS1.   KALLUNDBORG (1917)
O.N. 106638. 1590g, 1004n. 260.1 × 37.1 × 18.2 feet.
T.3-cyl. by Dunsmuir and Jackson, Glasgow.
3.6.1898: Launched by R. Duncan and Co. Ltd., Port Glasgow (Yard No. 281), as DENEWELL for George N. Patterson, Newcastle upon Tyne. *25.7.1898:* Delivered. *1899:* Registered under Northern Steamship Co. Ltd., (G. N. Patterson, manager). *6.1901:* Sold to Dampskibsselskabet Neptun (C. K. Hansen, manager), Denmark and renamed KALLUNDBORG. *19.4.1917:* Requisitioned by The Shipping Controller and registered under Sir Edward Hain at St. Ives. *5.6.1917:* Captured and sunk by German submarine about 80 miles S.W. of Toulon, while on a voyage from Genoa to Bougie in ballast.

MS2.   TAARNHOLM (1917 — 1918)
O.N. 137866. 1424g, 845n. 252.0 × 38.2 × 16.2 feet.
T.3-cyl. by North Eastern Marine Engineering Co. Ltd., Newcastle upon Tyne.
14.10.1905: Launched by Wood, Skinner and Co. Ltd., Newcastle upon Tyne, (Yard No. 128), for Dampskibsselskabet Steam (Johsen & Jespersen, managers), Denmark. *12.1905:* Completed. *1908:* Sold to Dampskibsselskabet Codan A/S (W. Schaldemose, manager), Denmark. *1912:* Sold to Akties Dampskibsselskabet Carl (L. H. Carl, manager), Denmark. *1917:* Requisitioned by The Shipping Controller and registered under Sir Edward Hain at St. Ives. *13.10.1917:* Foster, Hain and Read appointed managers. *1918:* Returned to former owners. *1919:* Sold to Det Forenede Dampskibsselskabet, Denmark. *1951:* Sold to Societa Armamento Marittima a.r.l. (SOARMA), Italy, and renamed ISA VIGO. *1954:* Sold to Nicola Guida, Italy, and renamed NUOVO ARNO. *1966:* Sold to Italian shipbreakers and arrived *19.5.1966* at Vado.

MS3.   ANTWERPEN (1917)
O.N. 137864. 1637g, 1098n. 264.0 × 35.1 × 16.6 feet.
T.3-cyl. by Wallsend Slipway Company, Newcastle upon Tyne.
1887: Launched by C. S. Swan and Hunter, Newcastle, (Yard No. 81), for Forenede Dampskibs Selskab, Denmark. *9.1887:* Completed. *1904:* Admiral A. de Richelieu appointed manager. *1907:* Management ceased. *1917:* Requisitioned by The Shipping Controller and registered under Sir Edward Hain at St. Ives. *13.10.1917:* Foster, Hain and Read appointed managers. *18.11.1917:* Torpedoed by the German submarine UC.77, S.W. of the Runnelstone Buoy in the English Channel, whilst on a voyage from Barry Dock to Rouen, with a cargo of coal. She was beached, but found to be beyond economical repair and abandoned as a total loss.

MS4.   DANEFAERD (1917 — 1918)
O.N. 137865. 1416g, 1031n. 248.8 × 33.1 × 15.5 feet.
C.2-cyl. by the Shipbuilders.
1884: Launched by Burmeister & Wain A/S, Copenhagen (Yard No. 129), as AMALIENBORG for Dampskibsselskabet Dannebrog (C. K. Hansen, manager), Denmark. *10.6.1884:* Delivered. *9.1916:* Sold to Dampskibsselskabet Oceana A/S (E. Harboe, manager), Denmark, and renamed DANEFAERD. *1917:* Requisitioned by The Shipping Controller. Foster, Hain and Read managers. *1918:* Returned to former owners. *1919:* Suenson & Jespersen appointed managers. *3.1925:* Sold to Leonidas Spinaris, Constantinos Koufopandelis and Leonidas Devedjiades (N. Tsouros, Spinaris and Co. managers), Greece, and renamed OMIROS. *1927:* S. D. Pandelis and Co. appointed managers. *11.8.1931:* Wrecked on an uncharted reef off the island of Skantsura whilst on a voyage from Galatz to Sulina, Volos, Piraeus and Nauplia with grain, timber and linseed.

VESSELS MANAGED ON BEHALF OF
THE MINISTRY OF WAR TRANSPORT

EMPIRE HEYWOOD as SAINT GREGORY

M1. EMPIRE HEYWOOD (1941 — 1944)
O.N. 166212. 7030g, 4967n. 431.3 (446.3 o.l.) × 56.3 × 35.2 feet.
T.3-cyl. by North Eastern Marine Engineering Co. (1938) Ltd., Newcastle.
21.10.1941: Launched by Caledon Shipbuilding and Engineering Co. Ltd., Dundee (Yard No. 393), for the Ministry of War Transport. The Hain Steamship Co. Ltd. appointed managers. *16.3.1942:* Completed. *29.1.1944:* The Saint Line Ltd., London appointed managers. *23.9.1947:* Sold to The Saint Line Ltd., London, and renamed SAINT GREGORY. *1962:* Sold to Stuart Navigation Co. (Bahamas) Ltd., Hong Kong, and renamed ANDROS. *1963:* Sold to The Escort Shipping Co. Ltd., (World-Wide [Shipping] Ltd., managers), Hong Kong and renamed ABIKO. *1966:* Sold to Pine S.S. Co. Ltd., Hong Kong. *22.3.1967:* Delivered to Lee Sing Company at Hong Kong for demolition and *31.3.1967* work commenced.

M2. EMPIRE RANGER (1941 — 1942)
O.N. 168978. 7008g, 4970n. 431.0 (446.0 o.l.) × 56.2 × 34.2 feet.
T.3-cyl. by J. G. Kincaid and Co. Ltd., Greenock.
3.12.1941: Launched by Lithgows Ltd., Port Glasgow (Yard No. 960), for the Ministry of War Transport. The Hain Steamship Co. Ltd. appointed managers. *22.1.1942:* Completed. *28.3.1942:* Bombed and sunk by German aircraft in the Arctic Ocean, N.E. of North Cape, in position 72.10 N, 30.00 E. She was on a voyage from Glasgow to North Russia with stores. Her crew of 56 were all taken prisoner of war.

M3. EMPIRE BEDE (1942)
O.N. 168709. 6959g, 4201n. 432.7 × 56.3 × 34.3 feet.
6-cyl. 4 S.C.S.A. Burmeister & Wain oil engine by the Shipbuilder.
6.1.1942: Launched by Harland and Wolff Ltd., Glasgow (Yard No. 1094G), for the Ministry of War Transport. The Hain Steamship Co. Ltd. appointed managers. *31.3.1942:* Completed. *18.8.1942:* Torpedoed by the German submarine U.553 in the North Atlantic in a position 19.35 N, 76.25 W, and subsequently sunk by H.M.S. PIMPERNEL in a position 19.41 N, 76.50 W. She was on a voyage from Alexandria and Trinidad to Key West and New York with a cargo of cotton. 2 of her crew of 43 were lost.

M4. OCEAN PEACE (1942 — 1943)
O.N. 168558. 7173g, 4278n. 425.1 (441.5 o.l.) × 57.0 × 34.8 feet.
T.3-cyl. by General Machinery Corporation, Hamilton, Ohio, U.S.A.
8.2.1942: Launched by Todd-Bath Iron Shipbuilding Corporation, Portland, Maine, U.S.A. (Yard No. 3), for the Ministry of War Transport. The Hain Steamship Co. Ltd. appointed managers. *3.4.1942:* Completed. *12.7.1943:* Bombed and sunk by Axis aircraft in the Central Mediterranean off Avola, Sicily, in a position 36.55 N, 15.13 E. She was on a voyage from Alexandria to Sicily with 3000 tons of military stores. Her crew was saved.

OCEAN PEACE

M5. OCEAN JUSTICE (1942)
O.N. 168632. 7173g, 4278n. 425.1 (441.5 o.l.) × 57.0 × 34.8 feet.
T.3-cyl. by General Machinery Corporation, Hamilton, Ohio, U.S.A.
8.2.1942: Launched by Todd-Bath Iron Shipbuilding Corporation, Portland, Maine, U.S.A. (Yard No. 4), for the Ministry of War Transport. The Hain Steamship Co. Ltd. appointed managers. *18.4.1942:* Completed. *6.11.1942:* Torpedoed by the German submarine U.505, E. of Trinidad in a position 10.06 N, 60.00 W. She was on a voyage from Karachi and Durban to Trinidad and New York with 600 tons of manganese ore as ballast. Her crew was saved.

M6. EMPIRE BOWMAN (1942 — 1943)
O.N. 168714. 7031g, 4967n. 431.3 (446.3 o.l.) × 56.3 × 35.2 feet.
T.3-cyl. by Barclay, Curle and Co. Ltd., Glasgow.
4.4.1942: Launched by C. Connell and Co. Ltd., Glasgow (Yard No. 437), for the Ministry of War Transport. The Hain Steamship Co. Ltd. appointed managers. *25.5.1942:* Completed. *30.3.1943:* Torpedoed and sunk by the German submarine U.404, S.W. of Cape Clear, in a position 47.26 N, 15.53 W. She was on a voyage from Karachi, Mormugao and Freetown to Hull with 8471 tons of general cargo, including 2500 tons of manganese ore. 4 of her crew of 44 and 6 gunners were lost.

M7. OCEAN COURAGE (1942 — 1943)
O.N. 168830. 7173g, 4278n. 425.1 (441.5 o.l.) × 57.0 × 34.8 feet.
T.3-cyl. by General Machinery Corporation, Hamilton, Ohio, U.S.A.
22.5.1942: Launched by Todd-Bath Iron Shipbuilding Corporation, South Portland, Maine, U.S.A. (Yard No. 10), for the Ministry of War Transport. The Hain Steamship Co. Ltd. appointed managers. *16.6.1942:* Completed. *15.1.1943:* Torpedoed and sunk by the German submarine U.182, S.W. of Bathurst, Gambia, in a position 10.52 N, 23.28 W. She was on a voyage from Pepel and Freetown to Trinidad and the U.K. with 9000 tons of iron ore and 8 bags of mail.

M8. FORT CEDAR LAKE (1942 — 1943)
7134g, 4244n. 424.6 (441.5 o.l.) × 57.2 × 34.9 feet.
T.3-cyl. by Canadian Allis-Chalmers Ltd., Montreal, Canada.
29.10.1942: Launched by North Van Shiprepairs Ltd., Vancouver, British Columbia, Canada (Yard No. 114), for the United States War Shipping Administration and bare-boat chartered to the Ministry of War Transport. The Hain Steamship Co. Ltd. appointed managers. *12.12.1942:* Completed. *17.3.1943:* Torpedoed by the German submarine U.338, S.E. of Cape Farewell, in a position 52.14 N, 32.15 W. She was later torpedoed again by the German submarine U.665 and sank. She was on a voyage from Vancouver and New York to Belfast Lough with general cargo. Her crew of 44 and 6 gunners were rescued.

EMPIRE CATO

M9. EMPIRE CATO (1942 — 1946)
O.N. 168949. 7039g, 4851n. 431.5 (446.3 o.l.) × 56.2 × 35.2 feet.
T.3-cyl. by Central Marine Engine Works, West Hartlepool.
10.11.1942: Launched by W. Gray and Co. Ltd., West Hartlepool (Yard No. 1138), for the Ministry of War Transport. The Hain Steamship Co. Ltd. appointed managers. *30.12.1942:* Completed. *12.4.1946:* Chartered to The Clan Line Steamers Ltd. for 3 years under the Ministry's Ship Disposal Scheme and delivered at 17.00 hours at Barrow-in-Furness. *31.12.1947:* Sold to The Clan Line Steamers Ltd., (Cayzer, Irvine and Co. Ltd., managers) Glasgow. *1948:* Renamed CLAN MACKENZIE. *1960:* Sold to Wheelock Marden and Co. Ltd. for demolition and arrived *14.10.1960* at Hong Kong. *11.1960:* Demolition commenced.

M10. FORT ANNE (1942 — 1946)
O.N. 168413. 7134g, 4244n. 424.6 (441.5 o.l.) × 57.2 × 34.9 feet.
T.3-cyl. by Dominion Engineering Works Ltd., Montreal, Canada.
18.11.1942: Launched by Burrard Dry Dock Co. Ltd., Vancouver, British Columbia, Canada (Yard No. 152), for the United States War Shipping Administration and bare-boat chartered to the Ministry of War Transport. The Hain Steamship Co. Ltd. appointed managers. *24.12.1942:* Completed. *18.5.1943:* Torpedoed by the German submarine U.414, W. of Algiers in a position 36.35 N, 01.01 E and abandoned by her crew. She was on a voyage from the River Tyne to Algiers with a cargo of military stores. Later reboarded by her crew, she arrived at Algiers *19.5.1943* and was then towed to Gibraltar for discharge and temporary repairs. Subsequently repaired at Middlesbrough and returned to service. *28.5.1946:* Lyle Shipping Co. Ltd., appointed managers. *9.4.1948:* Returned to the United States Maritime Commission. *1958:* Sold to Bethlehem Steel Co. for demolition and arrived *16.12.1958* at Baltimore. Work was undertaken by Patapsco Scrap Co.

EMPIRE CARPENTER as APEX   *Dr G. S. Wilson*

110

M11.   EMPIRE CARPENTER (1942 — 1944)
O.N. 168745. 7025g, 4857n. 431.3 (446.3 o.l.) × 56.3 × 35.2 feet.
T.3-cyl. by D. Rowan and Co. Ltd., Glasgow.
21.11.1942: Launched by C. Connell and Co. Ltd., Glasgow (Yard No. 440), for the Ministry of War Transport. The Hain Steamship Co. Ltd. appointed managers. *31.12.1942:* Completed. *25.4.1944:* Bare-boat chartered to the U.S.S.R. and renamed DICKSON. *14.11.1946:* Returned to the Ministry of Transport, renamed EMPIRE CARPENTER and laid up. *18.6.1947:* Sold to Petrinovic and Co. Ltd., London, and renamed PETFRANO. *1955:* Sold to Compania de Naviera Amipa S.A., Liberia, and renamed AMIPA. *1958:* Sold to Compania Naviera Apex S.A., Liberia and renamed APEX. *1968:* Renamed AFROS. *1970:* Sold to The Campos Shipping Co. Ltd., Cyprus. *1971:* Sold to Chinese shipbreakers and delivered *17.3.1971* at Shanghai.

FORT VERCHERES as MAPLE HILL   *Skyfotos*

M12.   FORT VERCHERES (1942 — 1946)
O.N. 168457. 7128g, 4239n. 424.5 (440.5 o.l.) × 57.2 × 34.9 feet.
T.3-cyl. by Dominion Engineering Works Ltd., Montreal, Canada.
5.12.1942: Launched by United Shipyards Ltd., Montreal, Canada (Yard No. 4), for the Dominion of Canada and bare-boat chartered to the Ministry of War Transport. The Hain Steamship Co. Ltd. appointed managers. *8.5.1943:* Completed. *13.8.1946:* Sub-chartered to Dalhousie Steam and Motorship Co. Ltd., London and delivered at noon at Rosario, Brazil. *1950:* Sold to Halifax Overseas Freighters Ltd. (Counties Ship Management Co. Ltd., managers), London and renamed MAPLE HILL. *1965:* Transferred to Counties Steam Navigation Co. Ltd. (Counties Shipping Ltd., managers), London. *1966:* Sold to Diopside Steamship (Panama) S.A., Panama, and renamed DIOPSIDE. *1969:* Renamed ENTAN. *1970:* Sold to Matsuhura Maritime Co. Ltd., Japan for demolition and work commenced *2.9.1970* at Hirao.

M13.   FORT JEMSEG (1942 — 1943)
O.N. 168423. 7134g, 4244n. 424.6 (441.5 o.l.) × 57.2 × 34.9 feet.
T.3-cyl. by John Inglis Co. Ltd., Toronto, Ontario, Canada.
17.12.1942: Launched by Burrard Dry Dock Co. Ltd., Vancouver, British Columbia, Canada (Yard No. 153), for the United States War Shipping Administration and bare-boat chartered to the Ministry of War Transport. The Hain Steamship Co. Ltd. appointed managers. *22.1.1943:* Completed. *23.9.1943:* Torpedoed and sunk by the German submarine U.238, S.E. of Cape Farewell, in a position 53.18 N, 40.24 W. She was on a voyage from Hull and Loch Ewe to New York in ballast. One of her crew of 54 was lost.

111

FORT CHESTERFIELD   *Welsh Industrial & Maritime Museum*

M14.   FORT CHESTERFIELD (1943 — 1946)
O.N. 168456. 7127g, 4248n. 424.6 (441.5 o.l.) × 57.2 × 34.9 feet.
T.3-cyl. by Canadian Allis-Chalmers Ltd., Montreal, Canada.
25.2.1943: Launched by Burrard Dry Dock Co. Ltd., Vancouver, British Columbia, Canada (Yard No. 162), for the United States War Shipping Administration and bare-boat chartered to the Ministry of War Transport. The Hain Steamship Co. Ltd. appointed managers. *27.3.1943:* Completed. *23.11.1946:* Sub-chartered to Goulandris Brothers Ltd. *29.11.1948:* Sold to G. and T. Shipping Ltd., Canada. *1949:* Sold to Societa Armadora del Norte, Panama, and renamed HAWK. *1954:* Sold to Compania Maritima del Este S.A., Panama. *1958:* Sold to Salinas Compania Naviera S.A., Panama. *1966:* Sold to Cabahamas Corporation Ltd., Bahamas, and renamed CABAHAWK. *1968:* Sold to Taiwan shipbreakers and arrived *30.3.1968* at Kaohsiung.

EMPIRE MACANDREW   *T. Rayner*

M15.   EMPIRE MACANDREW (1943 — 1946)
O.N. 168767. 7952g, 5219n. 429.8 × 56.3 × 34.2 feet.
6-cyl. 4 S.C.S.A. Burmeister & Wain oil engine by J. G. Kincaid and Co. Ltd., Greenock.
3.5.1943: Launched by W. Denny and Brothers Ltd., Dumbarton (Yard No. 1370), as a merchant aircraft carrier for the Ministry of War Transport. The Hain Steamship Co. Ltd. appointed managers. *7.7.1943:* Completed. *23.10.1946:* Sold to McCowen and Gross Ltd., London, and renamed DERRYHEEN. *1951:* Sold to Cape of Good Hope Motorship Co. Ltd. (Lyle Shipping Co. Ltd., managers), Glasgow, and renamed CAPE GRAFTON. *1954:* Registered under Lyle Shipping Co. Ltd. *1963:* Sold to Patricia Compania Naviera S.A., Liberia, and renamed PATRICIA. *1967:* Sold to Pomos Shipping Co. Ltd., Cyprus. *1970:* Sold to China National Machinery Import and Export Corporation for demolition and delivered 16.40 local time *4.10.1970* at Hsinkiang.

M16.   FORT BELLINGHAM (1943 — 1944)
O.N. 169627. 7153g, 4240n. 424.6 (441.5 o.l) × 57.2 × 34.9 feet.
T. 3-cyl. by Dominion Engineering Works Ltd., Montreal, Canada.
13.6.1943: Launched by Burrard Dry Dock Co. Ltd., Vancouver, British Columbia, Canada (Yard
No. 182), for the Dominion of Canada and bare-boat chartered to the Ministry of War Transport.
The Hain Steamship Co. Ltd. appointed managers. *18.8.1943:* Completed. *26.1.1944:* Torpedoed
and sunk by the German submarines U.360 and U.957 off North Cape, in a position 73.25 N,
25.10 E. She was on a voyage from London to Murmansk in Convoy JW.56A with 4800 tons
of military stores. 21 crew and 16 gunners plus two of the Commodore's staff were lost.

M17.   EMPIRE MACRAE (1943 — 1947)
O.N. 169507. 8252g, 5330n. 429.5 × 57.9 × 35.3 feet.
6-cyl. 4 S.C.S.A. Burmeister & Wain oil engine by J. G. Kincaid and Co. Ltd., Greenock.
21.6.1943: Launched by Lithgows Ltd., Port Glasgow (Yard No. 992), as a merchant aircraft
carrier for the Ministry of War Transport. The Hain Steamship Co. Ltd. appointed managers.
20.9.1943: Completed. *25.1.1947:* Sold to Moller Line Ltd., London, and subsequently renamed
ALPHA ZAMBESI. *1947:* Transferred to Alpha South African S.S. Co. Ltd. (Moller Line S.A. (Pty.)
Ltd., managers), London. *1949:* Sold to Motor Lines Ltd. (Clunies Shipping Company, managers),
Greenock. *1951:* Management ceased. *1953:* Sold to Westport Shipping Co. Ltd., London. *1954:*
Sold to Skibs. A/S Vilhelm Torkildsen's Rederi (Vilhelm Torkildsen, manager), Norway, and
renamed TOBON. *1957:* Sold to D/S A/S Flint & Skibs. A/S Vilhelm Torkildsen's Rederi (Erling
Torkildsen & Wollert Holst, managers), Norway. *1960:* Sold to D/S A/S Flint (Willy Kubon,
manager), Norway. *1967:* Sold to Aghiaparaskevi Corp., Greece, and renamed DESPINA P. *1971:*
Sold to Chi Shan Hwa Steel and Iron Works Co., Taiwan, for demolition and work commenced
2.5.1971 at Kaohsiung. *5.6.1971:* Demolition completed.

FORT BOISE

M18.   FORT BOISE (1943 — 1946)
O.N. 169926. 7151g, 4234n. 424.6 (439.3 o.l.) × 57.2 × 34.9 feet.
T. 3-cyl. by John Inglis Co. Ltd., Toronto, Canada.
21.7.1943: Launched by West Coast Shipbuilders Ltd., Vancouver, British Columbia, Canada
(Yard No. 127), for the Dominion of Canada and bare-boat chartered to the Ministry of War
Transport. The Hain Steamship Co. Ltd. appointed managers. *17.9.1943:* Completed. *22.5.1946:*
Returned to the Canadian Government. Park Steamship Co. Ltd. appointed managers. *23.8.1946:*
Ran aground on Grand Shoal, E. of St. Pierre, Miquelon Island, broke in two, and was abandoned
as a total loss. She was on a voyage from Botwood to Northern France with a cargo of
concentrates.

M19. FORT SAKISDAC (1943 — 1946)
O.N. 169945. 7160g, 4244n. 424.6 (441.5 o.l.) × 57.2 × 34.9 feet.
T. 3-cyl. by Dominion Engineering Works Ltd., Montreal, Canada.
31.7.1943: Launched by Burrard Dry Dock Co. Ltd., Vancouver, British Columbia, Canada (Yard No. 188), for the Dominion of Canada and bare-boat chartered to the Ministry of War Transport. The Hain Steamship Co. Ltd. appointed managers. *20.10.1943:* Completed. *12.9.1946:* Sold to Canadian Shipowners Ltd. (March Shipping Agency Ltd., managers), Canada, and renamed MARCHCAPE. *1948:* Montreal Shipping Co. Ltd. appointed managers. *1949:* Sold to Compania de Naviera Panamena Ultramarina S.A., Panama, and renamed MARGO. *1959:* Sold to Toula Navegacion Ltda., Panama, and renamed TOULA N. *1961:* Transferred to Lebanese registry. *1963:* Sold to Hong Kong Chiap Hua Mfy. Co. (1947) Ltd., Hong Kong, for demolition. *14.2.1963:* Demolition commenced.

EMPIRE MACCALLUM   *T. Rayner*

M20. EMPIRE MACCALLUM (1943 — 1947)
O.N. 169508. 8252g, 5330n. 429.5 × 57.9 × 35.3 feet.
6-cyl. 4 S.C.S.A. Burmeister & Wain oil engine by J. G. Kincaid and Co. Ltd., Greenock.
12.10.1943: Launched by Lithgows Ltd., Port Glasgow (Yard No. 993), as a merchant aircraft carrier for the Ministry of War Transport. The Hain Steamship Co. Ltd. appointed managers. *22.12.1943:* Completed. *1.10.1947:* Sold to Doris Steam Ship Co. Ltd. (Clunies Shipping Company, managers), Greenock, and renamed DORIS CLUNIES. *1951:* Renamed SUNROVER. *1953:* Dracoulis Ltd. appointed managers. *1957:* Renamed EUDOXIA. *1959:* Sold to Phorkyss Shipping Corporation, Greece, and renamed PHORKYSS. *28.5.1960:* Laid up in the River Blackwater and while lying there sold to Japanese shipbreakers. *10.11.1960:* Demolition commenced at Sakai City, Japan.

EMPIRE GENERAL as HENDONHALL

M21. EMPIRE GENERAL (1943 — 1947)
O.N. 180131. 7359g, 5008n. 431.0 (444.8 o.l.) × 56.5 × 35.5 feet.
3-cyl. 2 S.C.S.A. oil engine by the Shipbuilder.
11.11.1943: Launched by Wm. Doxford and Sons Ltd., Sunderland (Yard No. 712), for the Ministry of War Transport. The Hain Steamship Co. Ltd. appointed managers. *25.3.1944:* Completed. *5.2.1947:* Sold to The West Hartlepool Steam Navigation Co. Ltd., West Hartlepool,

and renamed HENDONHALL. *1958:* Sold to Lebanesa Ltda. S.A., Lebanon, and renamed TAXIARHIS. *1971:* Renamed TONY C. *1972:* Sold to Sidiremboriki, Greece, for demolition, which commenced *24.4.1972* at Skaramanga.

FORT LA HAVE   *Welsh Industrial & Maritime Museum*

M22.   FORT LA HAVE (1944 — 1946)
O.N. 169912. 7166g, 4242n. 424.6 (441.5 o.l.) × 57.2 × 34.9 feet.
T. 3-cyl. by Dominion Engineering Works Ltd., Montreal, Canada.
8.1.1944: Launched by Burrard Dry Dock Co. Ltd., Vancouver, British Columbia, Canada (Yard No. 202), for the Dominion of Canada and bare-boat chartered to the Ministry of War Transport. The Hain Steamship Co. Ltd. appointed managers. *8.3.1944:* Completed. *15.10.1946:* Returned to the Canadian Government. Park Steamship Co. Ltd. appointed managers. *1947:* Sold to Lunham and Moore (Canada) Ltd., Canada, and renamed ANGUSGLEN. *1948:* Registered under Lunham and Moore Steamships Ltd. (Lunham and Moore Shipping Ltd., managers). *1954:* Lyle Shipping Co. Ltd., Glasgow, appointed managers, transferred to British registry, and renamed CAPE MELAN. *1955:* Sold to A. C. Hadjipateras, Greece, registered Costa Rica and renamed AGHIOS SPYRIDON. *1959:* Transferred to Greek registry. *27.5.1959:* Went aground some 80 miles W. of Havana, Cuba, in a position 22.53 N, 83.48 W, whilst on passage from Hampton Roads to Japan. Fire later broke out in her engine room causing serious damage and she was abandoned by her crew. *19.6.1959:* Refloated and sold to Aquamarine Compania Naviera, Greece, who found her to be beyond economical repair. She was sold to the British Iron and Steel Corporation Ltd., loaded with scrap at U.S. Gulf ports and towed to the U.K. for discharge and demolition. Arrived *27.10.1960* at Ardrossan and moved round *23.11.1960* to Troon. *27.4.1961:* Demolition commenced by West of Scotland Shipbreaking Co. Ltd.

FORT ISLAND

M23.   FORT ISLAND (1944 — 1946)
O.N. 169867. 7167g, 4235n. 424.6 (441.5 o.l.) × 57.2 × 34.9 feet.
T. 3-cyl. by John Inglis Co. Ltd., Toronto, Canada.
22.1.1944: Launched by Burrard Dry Dock Co. Ltd., Vancouver, British Columbia, Canada (Yard No. 203), for the Dominion of Canada and bare-boat chartered to the Ministry of War Transport. The Hain Steamship Co. Ltd. appointed managers. *16.3.1944:* Completed. *1.6.1946:* Returned to the Canadian Government. Park Steamship Co. Ltd. appointed managers. *1946:* Sold to Montship Lines Ltd. (Montreal Shipping Co. Ltd., managers), Canada, and renamed MONT ROLLAND. *1949:* Sold to Gestioni Esercizio Navi-G.E.N., Italy, and renamed MARIA PAOLINA G. *1960:* Sold to "Aretusa" S.p.A. di Navigazione, Italy, for demolition, who contracted the work to Terrestre Marittima S.p.A., Spezia. *7.1960:* Demolition commenced.

115

EMPIRE MACDERMOTT as LA CUMBRE

M24. EMPIRE MACDERMOTT (1944 — 1947)
O.N. 169407. 7952g, 5224n. 429.8 × 56.3 × 34.2 feet.
6-cyl. 4 S.C.S.A. Burmeister & Wain oil engine by J. G. Kincaid and Co. Ltd., Greenock.
24.1.1944: Launched by W. Denny and Brothers Ltd., Dumbarton (Yard No. 1378), as a merchant aircraft carrier for the Ministry of War Transport. The Hain Steamship Co. Ltd. appointed managers. *31.3.1944:* Completed. *15.8.1947:* Sold to Buries Markes Ltd., London, and *1948* renamed LA CUMBRE. *1959:* Sold to Canero Compania Naviera S.A., Greece, and renamed PARNON. *1969:* Sold to Southern Shipping and Enterprises Co. Ltd., Somali Republic, and renamed STARLIGHT. *c.1976:* Transferred to China Ocean Shipping Co. Believed still in service.

SAMSPERRIN loading china clay at Fowey   *W.S.P.L.*

M25. SAMSPERRIN (1944 — 1947)
O.N. 169937. 7219g, 4380n. 422.8 × 57.0 × 34.8 feet.
T. 3-cyl. by Harrisburg Machinery Corporation, Harrisburg, Pennsylvania, U.S.A.
7.3.1944: Launched by New England Shipbuilding Corporation, Portland, Maine, U.S.A. (Yard No. 3005), for the United States War Shipping Administration and bare-boat chartered to the Ministry of War Transport. The Hain Steamship Co. Ltd. appointed managers. *18.3.1944:* Completed. *2.10.1947:* Returned to the United States Maritime Commission. *1951:* Registered under the United States Department of Commerce. *28.7.1961:* Sold to Union Minerals and Alloys Corporation, New York, and *11.1961* broken up at Panama City, Florida, U.S.A.

116

EMPIRE MANDARIN   *Welsh Industrial & Maritime Museum*

M26.   EMPIRE MANDARIN (1944 — 1946)
O.N. 169181. 7078g, 4875n. 430.9 (446.3 o.l.) × 56.2 × 35.2 feet.
T. 3-cyl. by North Eastern Marine Engineering Co. (1938) Ltd., Newcastle.
9.3.1944: Launched by the Shipbuilding Corporation Ltd. (Tyne Branch), Newcastle (Yard No. 7), for the Ministry of War Transport. The Hain Steamship Co. Ltd. appointed managers. *19.5.1944:* Completed. *24.4.1946:* Chartered to Dorset Steamship Co. Ltd. for five years under the Ministry's Ship Disposal Scheme and delivered at Lourenço Marques, Portuguese East Africa. *24.2.1947:* Sold to Dorset Steamship Co. Ltd. (Counties Ship Management Co. Ltd., managers), London, and renamed LULWORTH HILL. *1949:* Renamed CASTLE HILL. *2.1949:* Registered under London and Overseas Freighters Ltd. (Counties Ship Management Co. Ltd., managers). *1950:* Renamed LONDON BUILDER. *11.1950:* Sold to Societa Armadora Insular S.A., Panama, and renamed SILVER WAKE. *1954:* Sold to Eastern Seas Steamship Co. Ltd., London, and renamed NAVARINO. *1955:* Sold to Stanhope Steamship Co. Ltd. (J. A. Billmeir, later J. A. Billmeir and Co. Ltd., managers), London and renamed STANTHORPE. *1961:* Sold to Mullion and Co. Ltd., Hong Kong, and renamed ARDBRAE. *1966:* Sold to Koshin Sangyo K.K., Japan, for demolition and work commenced *14.3.1966* at Onomichi.

M27.   SAMSHEE (1944 — 1946)
O.N. 169956. 7210g, 4395n. 423.1 × 57.1 × 34.8 feet.
T. 3-cyl. by General Machinery Corporation, Hamilton, Ohio, U.S.A.
9.3.1944: Launched by Bethlehem-Fairfield Shipyard Inc., Baltimore, Maryland, U.S.A. (Yard No. 2338), for the United States War Shipping Administration and bare-boat chartered to the Ministry of War Transport. The Hain Steamship Co. Ltd. appointed managers. *21.3.1944:* Completed. *11.7.1946:* W. H. Seager and Co. Ltd., Cardiff, appointed managers. *11.6.1948:* Returned to the United States Maritime Commission. *1951:* Registered under the United States Department of Commerce. *26.2.1964:* Sold to Southern Scrap Material Co. Ltd. for demolition which oommenced *8.1964* at New Orleans, Louisiana, U.S.A.

SAMVIGNA   *Welsh Industrial & Maritime Museum*

M28. SAMVIGNA (1944 — 1948)
O.N. 169914. 7255g, 4372n. 422.8 × 57.0 × 34.8 feet.
T. 3-cyl. by General Machinery Corporation, Hamilton, Ohio, U.S.A.
8.4.1944: Launched by J. A. Jones Construction Co. Inc., Brunswick, Georgia, U.S.A. (Yard No.
138), for the United States War Shipping Administration and bare-boat chartered to the Ministry
of War Transport. The Hain Steamship Co. Ltd. appointed managers. *20.4.1944:* Completed.
28.6.1948: Returned to the United States Maritime Commission. *1951:* Registered under the
United States Department of Commerce. *18.2.1960:* Sold to Southern Scrap Material Co. Ltd.
for demolition which commenced *5.1960* at Mobile, Alabama, U.S.A.

M29. SAMADRE (1944 — 1947)
O.N. 169916. 7219g, 4380n. 422.8 × 57.0 × 34.8 feet.
T. 3-cyl. by General Machinery Corporation, Hamilton, Ohio, U.S.A.
4.1944: Launched by New England Shipbuilding Corporation, Portland, Maine, U.S.A. (Yard No.
3014), for the United States War Shipping Administration and bare-boat chartered to the Ministry
of War Transport. The Hain Steamship Co. Ltd. appointed managers. *15.5.1944:* Completed.
14.4.1947: Sold to Larrinaga Steamship Co. Ltd., Liverpool, and *13.6.1947* handed over and
renamed MARIA DE LARRINAGA. *1964:* Sold to Marseguro Compania Naviera S.A., Greece, and
renamed MELETIOS. *1969:* Sold to Japanese shipbreakers and arrived prior to *26.5.1969* at
Sakaide. *3.7.1969:* Demolition commenced.

M30. ROSEDALE PARK (1946)
O.N. 175388. 7139g, 4296n. 424.5 × 57.2 × 34.9 feet.
T. 3-cyl. by Dominion Engineering Works Ltd., Montreal.
29.3.1944: Launched by United Shipyards Ltd., Montreal (Yard No. 28), for the Canadian
Government. Park Steamship Co. Ltd. appointed managers. *25.5.1944:* Delivered. *12.9.1946:*
Bare-boat chartered to the Ministry of Transport. The Hain Steamship Co. Ltd. appointed
managers. *31.10.1946:* Weidner Hopkins and Company appointed managers. *18.2.1947:* St.
Quentin Shipping Co. Ltd. appointed managers. *8.3.1949:* William Brown, Atkinson and Co. Ltd.
appointed managers. *1950:* Sold to Halifax Overseas Freighters Ltd. (Counties Ship Management
Co. Ltd., managers), London, and renamed POPLAR HILL. *1960:* Sold to Dah Lien Shipping Co.
Ltd. (Shipping Managers (Hong Kong) Ltd., managers), Hong Kong, and renamed SHIENFOON.
1963: Jebmei Shipping Management Co. Ltd. appointed managers. *1968:* Sold to Mollers Ltd.,
Hong Kong, for demolition and *26.10.1968* delivered.

Text of a submission by Lord Inchcape to the P&O Board when the purchase of The Hain Steamship Co. Ltd. was under consideration.

I have had an offer of the Hain Steamship Company the fleet of which consists of 23 steamers with a deadweight capacity of 184,320 tons, the average tonnage age being eight years.

The vessels are high class cargo ships and would be very useful to us.

The offer is made on the basis of about £12 a ton on the deadweight capacity which brings their value to £1,972,392.

The company has cash assets of £2,400,000 and no Debentures or Preference shares and no liabilities except £400,000 for four vessels with a deadweight capacity of 31,680 tons under construction which are not included in the tonnage mentioned.

The purchase money provisionally agreed is £4,400,000. The offer provides for the profits of the company as from 1st July 1917 going to the purchasers. The steamers with the exception of two which are free from requisition and two which are interned in Germany will leave a profit of Blue Book rates of about £200,000 a year and the free steamers will leave a profit of probably £40,000 a year so long as they are free.

When the war is over the steamers will form a valuable adjunct to the P&O and British India companies and should make money.

I propose to leave the details of the working of the ships in the hands of the two men who now attend to them but associating them with Gray Dawes and Co. so that we shall have complete control.

I propose that we shall only buy the Hain Line provided we get 90% of the shares which, however, I am assured will be the case.

It is important to continue the Hain Line as a separate entity as the steamers are worked on more economical lines than either the P&O or British India Companies, the ships being of a different class and their Captains, Officers and Engineers being less highly paid, and worked in as regards coal, repairs etc. with the P&O and British India. I think considerable economies can be effected for all the fleets and it will be a material advantage for both the P&O and British India to have the call of these fine cargo ships after the war.

The Line has been very successfully worked in the past and there are considerable potentialities for the future.

The sale is proposed owing to the recent death of Sir Edward Hain the principal proprietor and the founder of the Line.

Sir Edward Hain's Trustees have considerable rights in connection with the Hain Steamship Company which will have to be satisfied, but the purchase money proposed includes provision for the satisfaction of the Trustees and this is a domestic matter which does not concern us.

It is proposed that Gray Dawes and Co. shall contribute £100,000 towards the purchase price in return for the accession of business which they will secure in the management of the Hain Steamship Company.

We can satisfy the purchase money to the extent of £2,400,000 out of the saleable investments consisting of War Loan, Treasury Bills, and Exchequer Bonds and the remaining £1,900,000 we can find without difficulty.

It is of course important that the proposed purchase should be kept absolutely secret.

THE MAC-SHIPS

Contributed by L. Sawyer

Merchant Aircraft Carriers were introduced into the wartime scene as a development of the earlier CAM-ships (Catapult-Armed Merchantmen), which were able to catapult a fighter aircraft but whose pilot had to be picked up after baling out, the aircraft being unable to return on to the ship.

After the collapse of France in mid-1940, groups of German Focke-Wulf 'Condor' long-range maritime reconnaissance bombers were stationed on the coast of the Bay of Biscay. They became an even-more valuable asset to the German war machine after the southern ports of Britain were closed to most merchant vessels and shipping was switched to northern ports, being routed as far out in the Atlantic as possible to escape the attentions of both the Luftwaffe and the coastal forces of the German Navy. But Allied ships could not escape quite so easily from some of Germany's capital ships and the U-boats nor from the 'Condors', whose range allowed them to reach far out into the Atlantic, beyond the limits of any aircraft based in the British Isles.

In operation the 'Condors' flew in a wide arc, looking for targets. There were plenty: despite the losses, more than two million tons of shipping was being turned round in British ports each month. Much of it sailed in convoy, even then its only air defence was the anti-aircraft guns of the few small vessels which could be spared as escorts.

Early versions of the 'Condor' carried four, sometimes five, 250-kilo (551 lb) bombs. The planes normally attacked at masthead height, usually dropping all their bombs in one stick, on one ship. Several might miss, generally at least one would find the target.

Convoys were routed even further west, but this only widened the gap between possible air cover from Gibraltar and that from Britain.

It became obvious that effective protection of shipping could only come from ship-borne fighter planes. But the Royal Navy could offer no assistance, its resources already stretched to breaking point.

In October 1940 the prototype of a Hawker 'Hurricane' (Mark I) land-based fighter, modified for marine catapult work, were ordered. Three months later sets of catapult equipment for 50 merchantmen were ordered and a start made on selecting the ships to be fitted. Work commenced on 35 vessels, at Bristol, Cardiff, Clydeside and Liverpool.

The vessels were to be called Catapult Aircraft-armed Merchant ships (CAM-ships), would carry normal cargoes and sail as parts of convoys. The first was the new vessel MICHAEL E. 7,628/41, owned by Counties Ship Management Ltd. which put to sea on 27th May 1941. There was no necessity to launch her plane in the North Atlantic danger zone and when only six days out she was torpedoed and sunk by the German submarine U.108.

In addition to the CAM-ships and their R.A.F. pilots, the Admiralty also found five ships that could be spared. The ARIGUANI 6,746/26 and PATIA 5,355/22, (both owned by Elders & Fyffes Ltd.) and the MAPLIN (ex ERIN) 5,824/32, owned by the Morant S.S.Co (Standard Fruit Corporation) but operated by Elders & Fyffes were awaiting conversion to Ocean Boarding Ships and the SPRINGBANK, 5,155/26, (Andrew Weir & Co.) was already converting to an anti-aircraft ship. Each was equipped with a catapult and fighter plane. The fifth vessel, the old Seaplane carrier PEGASUS, was taken off catapult trials and training and given three Fulmar fighters.

The five, known as Fighter Catapult Ships, would not carry cargo and would work as part of a convoy escort. The PEGASUS joined an outward bound convoy in December 1940. By April 1941 the remaining quartet was ready, although the PATIA was sunk off the Tyne by bombing just after completion. Of the remaining four, two were placed on the Gibraltar run and two in North Atlantic service.

Strangely, though, many of the first CAM-ships to put to sea reported no contacts with enemy aircraft; the first successful attack on a Focke-Wulf 'Condor' being by the 'Sea Hurricane' from the Fighter Catapult Ship MAPLIN on 3rd August 1941.

Nevertheless, sinkings had continued unabated. In the air alone, during the six months from August 1940, 'Condor' bombers from their air base at Bordeaux-Merignac sank 85 Allied ships totalling some 363,000 tons, whilst in the year up to Ju—e 1941, German planes sank, in total, more than a million tons of Allied shipping.

Despite this, the catapult-launched fighters proved their worth, providing some air cover and defence to convoys, particularly in a 500-mile gap of undefended air space in mid-Atlantic. But the fact that each fighter could make only one sortie was expensive and wasteful both in planes and, too often, in pilots as well. Launchings could not be carried out in rough weather nor could a judgement be made as to which incident might be 'the best' in which to use the fighter. Once it had been launched — and ditched — subsequent and, perhaps, more serious incidents were devoid of the very cover it was the intention to provide.

Merchant Ship Aircraft Carriers (MAC-ships) overcame this disadvantage, but were confined to two types, the grain carrier and the tanker. Their development stemmed from Admiralty discussions held at the time of the concept of the new-type 'Escort' carrier. By the early part of 1942 a dozen or so of these were on order, but their delivery was still very much into the future and, even so, they had already been committed elsewhere.

In this situationOit was decided to convert two grain-carrying ships to Merchant Aircraft Carriers — vessels which could operate aircraft yet continue to carry cargo.

The Burntisland Shipbuilding Co. was instructed to draw up the plans and to carry out conversion work. The Admiralty suggested a minimum flight deck length of 490 feet and a speed of some 15 knots, but it had to lower its sights to 390 feet and 12 knots to enable war-built, standard 'Empire'-type hulls of around 8-9,000 tons to be used.

The vessels selected were to be fitted with a hangar, aircraft-operating equipment and a flight deck and as their normal loading method was by flexible pipe or spout, there was no above-deck cargo-handling gear to impede this.

Soon after, in March 1942, it was urged that tankers which loaded in similar fashion, should also be converted. For a time the Admiralty and the Ministry of War Transport objected, mainly on the grounds of the fire risk involved, arguing that a valuable ship and cargo might be lost — yet disregarding the fact that this fate might await any loaded tanker in wartime, anyway, whether she carried aircraft and a flight deck, or not. In October 1942, when shipping losses were growing ever more serious, the grain ship conversion programme was expanded to six vessels and it was decided to convert six tankers as well, four of them 'Empire'-types still under construction and two Anglo-Saxon Petroleum Co. ships already in service.

Plans for the tanker conversions were prepared by Anglo-Saxon's own staff and although the selected ships were larger than the grain ships, thus giving a longer flight deck, the advantage was lost because there was no room for a hangar in the after structure. Four aircraft of the Fairey 'Swordfish' torpedo-spotter-reconnaissance type were to be carried on each grain ship, the planes being lowered into the hangar by lift. With the tankers only three similar planes could be carried and they would have to be parked on the after end of the flight deck.

EMPIRE MACKAY

Fleet Air Arm Museum

EMPIRE MACRAE *T. Rayner*

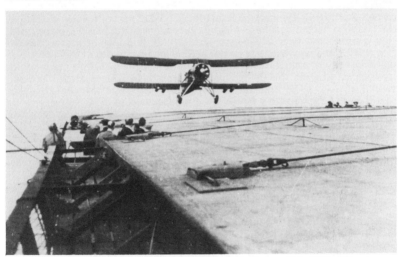

Swordfish aircraft landing on **EMPIRE MACALPINE.** This photograph is believed
to show the first landing of an aircraft on a "MAC" ship *Fleet Air Arm Museum*

EMPIRE MACCABE *Fleet Air Arm Museum*

The last six months of 1942 and the first ones of 1943, with MAC-ships still in dockyard hands, saw both sides suffering staggering losses in the Battle of the Atlantic.

In November 1942 U-boats sank over 700,000 tons of Allied shipping: in fact in the four months from August to November more than two million tons had been sunk. Two months of continuous gales eased the attacks, but in February the offensive was resumed, and . . . 'the Germans', says the official record, 'never came so near to disrupting communications between the New World and the Old as in the first 20 days of March 1943'. Forty-one ships were sunk in the first ten days, 56 in the second ten days — a total of more than half-a-million tons, of which some two-thirds was sunk in convoy. By this time, however, U-boat losses were almost matching their rate of construction and in May more than 40 were sunk.

At the same time the German 'Condor' bombers returned to the Biscay coast from the Russian Front, but now the routine patrols were carried out by Junkers 290's, the 'Condors' taking off only when a target had been sighted. Low-level attacks were forbidden, but with the use of radar frequent hits were scored in 'blind' bombing from the minimum of 9,000 feet.

The first MAC-ship, the grain carrier EMPIRE MACALPINE, commissioned on 14th April 1943. Her cargo was carried in holds fitted with flush, watertight hatches. The hangar, just large enough to accommodate her four planes with their wings folded, was served by a 42 feet × 20 feet lift. The first successful 'Swordfish' landing was made on her in May and at the end of the month she sailed in convoy, still classed as a merchant ship. The second grain carrier conversion, EMPIRE MACANDREW (converted by Denny Bros.) entered service in July 1943 and in the same month the first MAC-ship tanker conversion, Anglo-Saxon's RAPANA commissioned, after a conversion by Smith's Dock Co., North Shields, lasting only five months. Her flight deck was 461 feet in length — some 40 feet more than with the grain ships — but this 'extra' was lost by having planes always stored there and an added disadvantage was of having to man-handle parked planes forward, out of the way, every time a plane came over the stern, for landing. The RAPANA was, in fact, the first of nine Anglo-Saxon (now Shell) tankers to take up the MAC-ship status.

By this time, with MAC-ships and escort carriers coming into service, the Royal Navy's Fighter Catapult Ships had vanished from the convoy escort scene, the SPRINGBANK having been lost in September 1941 and the ARGIGUANI and MAPLIN returned to trade due to the shortage of refrigerated vessels.

In June 1943 the order went out to disband the CAM-ship association of the R.A.F. with the Merchant Navy. At the time five CAM-ships were still in service and the last two were expected back in the U.K. by early July. As it happened they — EMPIRE TIDE and EMPIRE DARWIN — did not leave Gibraltar until the 23rd of the month. They produced an excellent swansong, for on the 28th, when their convoy was out of range of any Allied air cover, three Focke-Wulf 'Condor' planes were shot down.

In September 1943 two more MAC's entered service, the grain ship EMPIRE MACREA, converted by Lithgow's and another Anglo-Saxon tanker conversion by Smith's Dock, the AMASTRA. The next month three more MAC's were completed, the tankers ANCYLUS and ACAVUS and the EMPIRE MACKAY, converted by Harland & Wolff at Govan. Now a total of eight MAC-ships were operational. A ninth vessel, EMPIRE MACCOLL, joined the fleet in November. A new vessel, she was converted while still building at the Cammell Laird shipyard.

The momentum of deliveries increased in the last month of the year, when five more were made. Three were converted tankers, Anglo-Saxon's ALEXIA, the EMPIRE MACCABE and the EMPIRE MACMAHON, converted by the Swan,

ALEXIA   *Fleet Air Arm Museum*

Hunter yard and two were dry cargo conversions, the EMPIRE MACCALLUM (Lithgow's) and the EMPIRE MACKENDRICK (Burntisland).

By early 1944 the German offensive in the Atlantic had been badly blunted and in the January/February two furdher MAC's, the tanker conversions ADULA and MIRALDA went into service, bringing the number of operational ones to sixteen. The MAC-type ships then gained the responsibility of giving continuous air cover to many North American convoys, providing each with at least one vessel. In the following month the EMPIRE MACDERMOTT (converted by Denny's) and the tanker GADILLA (Smith's Dock) were added. As well as it now being possible to place two or three MAC's with each convoy — their aircraft sufficient to police those particular sealanes and so leave the now-numerous escort carriers to operate elsewhere — the tanker-type MAC-ships were used to ferry aircraft from the U.S.A. to the U.K. in preparation for the invasion of Normandy. Eleven special voyages were made, bringing more than 200 aircraft.

The nineteenth and last MAC-ship entered service during May 1944. This was the Anglo-Saxon tanker MACOMA. Thirteen further conversions of tanker to MAC-ship had been planned, but the situation was such that these were not carried out.

On 21st May 1945, Squadron 836, the largest squadron in the Fleet Air Arm and the last to fly 'Swordfish' aircraft, was disbanded.

As each MAC-ship had neared completion a new flight for the squadron had been formed. Each was allocated a letter of the alphabet: it reached as far as the letter 'S', 19 flights in all, a total of 63 air crews.

On 28th June 1945 MAC-ships came to an end with the arrival in the U.K. of the EMPIRE MACKAY.

In all, Merchant Aircraft Carriers had made more than 170 round trips with Atlantic convoys and, in addition, had returned home on each trip carrying some 10,000 tons of grain or oil, supplies which were of the utmost importance to the war effort.

APPENDIX III

Hain vessels laid up in the River Fal from 1930-1963

Name	Date of arrival	Date of sailing
TREVORIAN	3. 3.1930	9. 8.1934
TREFUSIS	6. 3.1930	22.11.1934
TREMATON	9. 3.1930	11. 4.1931
TREWORLAS	11. 3.1930	6. 5.1931
TRECARNE	13. 3.1930	7.12.1933
MIN	13. 3.1930	8. 5.1931
TREBARTHA	16. 3.1930	27.11.1931
TREGANTLE	21. 3.1930	8.11.1934
FOYLE	22. 3.1930	21. 9.1934
TREMEADOW	24. 3.1930	27. 8.1930
TREDINNICK	29. 3.1930	28. 8.1934
TREGONNELL	25. 3.1930	9. 8.1935
TREGARTHEN	14. 4.1930	8. 3.1933
TREMORVAH	20. 4.1930	31. 8.1930
TREWIDDEN	14. 7.1930	30. 9.1931
TREWYN	14. 4.1931	14. 6.1935
TRELYON	6. 5.1931	28. 5.1935
TREWELLARD	30.11.1931	23. 3.1933
TRELOSKE	2. 1.1932	17. 9.1934
TREVETHOE	28.11.1958	11. 2.1959
TREGENNA	10. 4.1959	28. 7.1959
TREGOTHNAN	27. 7.1959	30.10.1959
TRELAWNY	13. 8.1962	4. 6.1963
TREWELLARD	16. 8.1962	28. 9.1962
TRELEVAN	25. 8.1962	13. 5.1963
TRELOSKE	1. 9.1962	21. 2.1963
TRELYON	24. 9.1962	4. 3.1963
TREMAYNE	4. 3.1963	21. 8.1963

FOYLE and other Hain vessels laid up in the River Fal
in the early 1930s   *K. O'Donoghue Collection*

A Hain vessel, believed to be **TREGLISSON,** loading coal in Barry
Dock c.1906   *K. O'Donoghue Collection*

APPENDIX IV

SELECTED FINANCIAL RESULTS

The profit figures below are taken from surviving company minute books. That for the
years 1902-1917 is described as gross profit and later years represent the profit on
voyages. This is the voyage profits of the fleet less the cost of repairs, surveys, cost
of lay up etc. Both sets of figures graphically demonstrate the volatile nature of the
freight markets, resulting in considerable variations in profits from year to year. The
years ended March 1931 and 1932 produced losses on voyages, two of only very few
that the company experienced.

Year ended		Year ended	
30.6.1902	£38,908	31.3.1929	£192,729
30.6.1903	£54,589	31.3.1930	£80,937
30.6.1904	£62,370	31.3.1931	(£84,093)
30.6.1905	£55,051	31.3.1932	(£35,322)
30.6.1906	£80,679	31.3.1933	£35,986
30.6.1907	£87,322	31.3.1935	£55,261
30.6.1908	£78,582	31.3.1937	£226,303
30.6.1909	£33,340	31.3.1938	£656,422
30.6.1910	£56,163	30.9.1948	£63,218
30.6.1911	£106,630	30.9.1950	£316,288
30.6.1912	£144,490	30.9.1952	£1,220,028
30.6.1913	£355,408	30.9.1954	£230,929
30.6.1914	£153,156	30.9.1956	£685,585
30.6.1915	£323,924	30.9.1958	£220,445
30.6.1916	£514,485	30.9.1960	£32,704
30.6.1917	£252,527	30.9.1962	£227,162

APPENDIX V
NOMENCLATURE

With the introduction of his first steamship, Edward Hain decided that it was time to standardise the naming system of his fleet. In electing to use the prefix 'TRE' meaning 'the place of', homestead or dwelling place, he was able to utilise the names of a wide variety of Cornish villages and farms, and also some of the county's noted families and their estates. Although meanings of the 56 separate names used are given below, in some cases there is disagreement about the translation from the old Cornish language. Where applicable, the location of the place is also given.

TREBARTHA HALL   *K. Ingram Collection*

TREBARTHA	'A place of baths or washing fountains' or 'A place of clubs or bats' An ancient residence in North Hill, a few miles north of Liskeard, for many years the residence of the Rodd family. Demolished in the 1950s.
TRECARNE	'Dwelling on the rocks' A farm near Camelford, North Cornwall.
TRECARRELL	'The place of the carl or chief' An old house in the parish of Lezant, seat of the Trecarrell family from before the Norman conquest until 1540.
TREDENHAM	'The place of a great man' A small manor in the parish of Probus near Truro.
TREDINNICK	'The place on a hill near a river' The residence of the Tredinnick family in North Cornwall.
TREFUSIS	'A fortified place' The residence of the Trefusis family in Mylor opposite Falmouth.
TREGANTLE	'A place of temptation' The name of two farms near Lanlivery, west of Lostwithiel.
TREGARTHEN	'The habitation in a garth or enclosure' The residence of the Tregarthen family in Gorran near Mevagissey.
TREGENNA	'The place of a ravine' The former residence of the Tregenna family in St. Ives, which later gave its name to Tregenna Castle, residence of the Stephens family and now the Tregenna Castle Hotel.
TREGLISSON	'The green place' The residence of the Nichols family in Phillack, Hayle
TREGONNELL	'The place of a channel' The Gannel is the name of an inlet and river mouth at Crantock, near Newquay.
TREGOTHNAN	'Old farm or town in the valley' The residence of the Boscawan family in the parish of St. Michael Penkivel near Falmouth.
TREGURNO	'The place of Cornwall' A farm in Buryan, west of Penzance.
TREHAWKE	'The place of the Hawke' Former residence of a family of this name in Liskeard.
TREKIEVE	'The place away from damp' A farm in St. Cleer, north west of Liskeard.
TRELAWNY	'The bushy place' or 'The place of oak' For some time the residence of the Bodrigans in the parish of Pelynt, west of Looe. Later the seat of the Trelawny family.
TRELEVAN	'The level place' The residence of the Trewoola family in Mevagissey.

TRELISSICK	'A dwelling on the broad creek' or 'The muddy place' A manor extending along the west bank of the River Fal in the parish of Feock.
TRELOSKE	'The place by the burnt land' The residence of the Trelask family in Lewannick near Liskeard.

TRELOYHAN MANOR   *K. Ingram Collection*

TRELYON	'The place of the legion' A village near St. Ives, originally spelt Treloyhan. This name, in the latter spelling, was adopted by Edward Hain for the residence he built for himself in St. Ives in 1892.
TREMATON	'The place of a great wave' A castle and manor in the parish of St. Stephens-by-Saltash formerly a residence of the Earls of Cornwall.
TREMAYNE	'The place at the stone' An ancient residence of a family of that name in Meneage on the south bank of the Helford River.
TREMEADOW	'The place of the meadow' A farm near Churchtown, St. Ives, sometimes spelt Tremeader.
TREMERE	'The place of a pool' At one time the residence of a family of that name in Lanivet, south west of Bodmin.
TREMORVAH	'The place by the sea shore' A residence in Truro, originally of the Bickford-Smith family, later of the shipowner R. B. Chellew, and now the property of the Ministry of Agriculture.
TRENEGLOS	'The place of a firm church' A small parish near Camelford, with a remote church set in beautiful countryside.
TRESILLIAN	'The sunny place' A small village on the Tresillian River near Truro, at the main entrance to the Tregothnan Estate.
TRESITHNEY	'The place of Sezni' (a saint's name) A farm in St. Columb Major, east of Newquay.
TREVALGAN	'The place of a mighty prince' The name of a farm and hill near St. Ives.
TREVANION	'The dwelling in a hollow' The name of an eminent family, living once on the site of the present Carhays Castle, in St. Michael Carhays, near Mevagissey.
TREVARRACK	'The place of the rock in the brook' A small hamlet below Trencrom Hill, near St. Ives.
TREVAYLOR	'The house of the workman' Modified spelling of Trevayler Mansion in Gulval, near Penzance.
TREVEAL	'The habitation by the river' Modified spelling of Trevail, a hamlet between Zennor and St. Ives.
TREVEAN	'The little house' A chapel, cove and hamlet at Perranuthnoe near Marazion.
TREVELLOE	'The sweet place' A farm in Paul, Penzance.
TREVELYAN	'The mill house' The ancient residence of the family of that name in St. Veep.

TREVERBYN	'The place of herbs or roots' The ancient manor (once spelt Treverbin) and one time residence of a family by that name in St. Austell.
TREVESSA	'The town of the second chief or Mael' A hamlet below Trevalgan Hill, near St. Ives.
TREVETHOE	'The place of the graves or tombs' A house in Lelant, at one time spelt Trevethow, and for many years the seat of the Praed and Tyringham families.
TREVIDER	'The place of eagles' A farm in St. Buryan, west of Penzance.
TREVILLEY	'The place of primroses' A farm in Sennen.

TREVINCE   *K. Ingram Collection*

TREVINCE	'The place by the track' A farm in Gwennap, south east of Redruth, at one time spelt Trefyns.
TREVITHICK	'The rustic or farmer's town' A house in St. Columb Major for many years the residence of the Arundell family.
TREVORIAN	'The place near the sea' A farm at Sennen near Land's End.
TREVOSE	'The place by the ditch' Trevose Head near St. Merryn, Padstow.
TREWAVAS	'The wintry place' Trewavas Head in Mount's Bay, near Porthleven.
TREWELLARD	'The place of good prospect' A manor in St. Just, near Land's End.
TREWIDDEN	'The white place' The Bolitho family house near Penzance. The first Hain steamer was so named in recognition of the help given by this banking family.
TREWINNARD	'The high, haughty or beloved town' or 'The town on the marsh' The ancient residence of the family of this name in St. Erth near the Hayle River.
TREWORLAS	'The house of Gorlois' A farm in Philleigh close to the River Fal.
TREWYN	'The fair place, or place of innocence' A house in St. Ives, formerly occupied by the Trewhella family.

In addition, three TRE names were invented in 1936 in order to preserve the uniformity of the fleet naming system.

TREHATA	A derivation of the original name NOHATA, which is an Indian town.
TREMINNARD	A derivation of the original name MIN, which is a Russian river.
TREMODA	A derivation of the original name NIMODA, which is an Indian town.

Other vessels built for the company were

BANGALORE	The administrative centre of the Indian State of Mysore.
BEHAR	A modified spelling of Bihar, an Indian state, west of Bengal.
BHUTAN	An independent state in the Himalayas, between Tibet and Assam.
BURDWAN	A town in Bengal, India.
GLYNN	A long beautiful valley in Cornwall.
MARGARET HAIN	The wife of Edward Hain the second.
MYSTERY	It was said that it was a mystery where the money would come from to pay for this vessel when she was ordered.
T.S.B	Thomas Simon Bolitho.

INDEX OF SHIPS

TREVAYLOR (II)	59	TREVETHOE (II)	60	TREVOSE (II)	30
TREVAYLOR (III)	119	TREVETHOE (III)	120	TREVOSE (III)	72
TREVAYLOR (IV)	147	TREVETHOE (IV)	131	TREVOSE (IV)	132
TREVEAL (I)	52	TREVIDER (I)	8	TREWAVAS	15
TREVEAL (II)	84	TREVIDER (II)	36	TREWELLARD (I)	16
TREVEAN (I)	12	TREVIDER (III)	62	TREWELLARD (II)	64
TREVEAN (II)	38	TREVIDER (IV)	130	TREWELLARD (III)	115
TREVEAN (III)	75	TREVILLEY (I)	3	TREWELLARD (IV)	128
TREVEAN (IV)	134	TREVILLEY (II)	31	TREWIDDEN (I)	1
TREVELLOE	10	TREVILLEY (III)	61	TREWIDDEN (II)	24
TREVELYAN (I)	27	TREVILLEY (IV)	121	TREWIDDEN (III)	69
TREVELYAN (II)	80	TREVINCE (I)	50	TREWIDDEN (IV)	127
TREVELYAN (III)	122	TREVINCE (II)	124	TREWIDDEN (V)	149
TREVERBYN (I)	53	TREVITHICK	98	TREWINNARD	99
TREVERBYN (II)	89	TREVORIAN (I)	17	TREWORLAS (I)	101
TREVESSA (I)	35	TREVORIAN (II)	54	TREWORLAS (II)	129
TREVESSA (II)	93	TREVORIAN (III)	91	TREWYN (I)	40
TREVETHOE (I)	28	TREVOSE (I)	6	TREWYN (II)	90

Hain vessels at anchor in Grand Harbour, Valetta   *M. Cassar*

The World Ship Society

The World Ship Society was founded in 1947 and has grown to become the leading organisation for all who are interested in ships. The Society publishes a monthly journal, 'Marine News', featuring the latest news of the world's merchant ships, warships and auxiliaries, together with articles on a wide range of subjects. The World Ship Photo Library is a major source of ship photographs, and the Society's Central Record is a unique and accessible source of information on ships back to 1830. The Society regularly publishes original works by members, frequently compiled and illustrated with the help of these archives. For details of the Society and a sample copy of 'Marine News', send 23p in stamps or four international reply coupons to Dept. (H), 58 Bicton Street, Exmouth, Devon EX8 2RU, U.K.